LANGUAGE AND LITERACY SERIES

Dorothy S. Strickland and Celia Genishi, Series Editors

Third Edition

The CHILD as CRITIC

TEACHING LITERATURE IN ELEMENTARY AND MIDDLE SCHOOLS

Glenna Davis Sloan

Teachers College, Columbia University
New York and London

Published by Teachers College Press, 1234 Amsterdam Avenue
New York, NY 10027

Grateful acknowledgment is offered to the following for permission to
reprint the poems indicated:

"Dark Girl" from *Personals* by Arna Bontemps. Copyright 1963 by
Arna Bontemps. Reprinted by permission of Harold Ober Associates,
Inc.

"In Time of Silver Rain" from *Selected Poems of Langston Hughes.*
Copyright 1938, renewed 1966 by Langston Hughes. Reprinted by
permission of Alfred A. Knopf, Inc.

"The Goblin" from *Picture Rhymes from Foreign Lands* by Rose Fyleman
(J. B. Lippincott). Copyright 1935, renewed 1963 by Rose Fyleman.
Reprinted by permission of HarperCollins Publishers, Inc.

The original edition of this work appeared under the title *The Child as
Critic: Teaching Literature in the Elementary School.* Copyright ©
1975 by Teachers College, Columbia University.

Library of Congress Cataloging-in-Publication Data

Sloan, Glenna Davis.
    The child as critic : teaching literature in elementary and middle
schools / Glenna Davis Sloan. —3rd ed.
       p.   cm. — (Language and literacy series : v. 5)
    Includes bibliographical references and index.
    ISBN 0-8077-3156-0.—ISBN 0-8077-3110-2 (pbk.)
    1. Literature—Study and teaching (Elementary)   2. Language arts
(Elementary) I. Title. II. Series.
LB1575.S53   1991
372.6'4—dc20   91-23980
                                                   CIP

ISBN 0-8077-3156-0
ISBN 0-8077-3110-2 (pbk.)

Printed on acid-free paper

Manufactured in the United States of America

98 97 96   4 3 2

To Jake, Charles and Mark

Contents

Foreword
to the Third Edition

Being human involves communication, usually through language, and the process of becoming a communicator begins when life begins—in every individual and in every culture. But for human beings to participate fully in a modern, technological society, their acquisition of language *and* literacy is a vital prerequisite. Skilled communication, both spoken and written, enables the effective functioning of our democratic institutions and our continued international competitiveness. The broad societal motives that compel us toward communicative competence, however, are not more powerful than individual and personal ones—those that result in a child's question, a mother's song, a teacher's lesson, a lover's poem. It is the importance of human communication in every aspect of our lives, from the global and societal to the intimate and personal, that makes language and literacy such fascinating topics of inquiry.

The Language and Literacy Series, of which the third edition of *The Child as Critic* is a part, is a broadly-based collection reporting on innovative theory, research, and practice in the various areas of language studies. Included are books on elementary and secondary reading and writing, literature study, language arts, high school and college English, early literacy, adult literacy, English as a Second Language, learning disabilities, and technology. The series explores the complex interrelationships among the individual, society, and language, both spoken and written. It is our hope that each selection in this series will be a significant addition to the knowledge base and understanding of what it means to acquire language and literacy.

One of the most powerful tools for language and literacy learning is exposure to good literature. Studies of children who enter school already reading and writing reveal that they have had vast experience with literature at home. They are familiar with a wide range of favorite books, and they invariably attempt to read and write with enthusiasm. Shared book experiences in school have an equally positive influence on young children's reading and writing. Similarly, the relationship between older students' personal enjoyment of books and their achievement in language and literacy is well documented.

Yet, with all that is known about the importance of children's literature, it is a relatively recent topic of scholarly research. And, although children's books have always been a part of the school curriculum, it has only been in recent years that trade books (as opposed to textbooks) have been regarded as foundational to the teaching of literacy and to the study of subjects across the school curriculum. Today's teachers are rethinking their literacy programs in order to offer their students more high-quality literary experiences. Never before have English language arts teachers been so eager to move away from skill sheets and pre-packaged programs toward more wholistic, literature-based approaches. This new enthusiasm for literature, however, has produced new challenges in the classroom. Many teachers have felt a sense of uneasiness and bewilderment as they attempt to replace old practices with new. They soon discover that undertaking new activities in the absence of a clear conception of the theoretical principles that support them can cause inconsistencies and contradictions in instruction. Thus, as teachers embrace these new approaches, their need to know and understand the use of literature in the classroom has never been greater. *The Child as Critic* offers them exactly what they want and need to know.

While Glenna Davis Sloan's previous editions of *The Child as Critic* have illuminated the field for many years, this third edition has the power and promise to help teachers develop a philosophical and practical construct of literature as *the* language art through which all other language arts (listening, speaking, reading, and writing) develop. Sloan's expert blend of theory and practice not only informs practitioners about how to bring literature into the lives of children, but it also helps them know why. *The Child as Critic* is based on sound theoretical principles of language acquisition and the reading and writing processes, and on current beliefs about language teaching, learning, and curriculum.

Sloan suggests that we are all in the process of becoming literate. *The Child as Critic* is a must-read for every teacher who wishes to nurture that process in children. It is a book for those who wish to go beyond merely teaching young learners to read and write to fostering competency and joy in language and literacy.

DOROTHY S. STRICKLAND AND CELIA GENISHI
Series Editors

Foreword to the First Edition

This book is an attempt to explain what the real place of literature is in primary education. Its place is to provide the verbal element in the training of the imagination. The imagination is not a self-indulgent, ornamental, or escapist faculty: It is the constructive power of the mind. Hence one should teach reading neither efficiently nor passively: Reading has to be a continuously active and leisurely growth, as is all genuine growth. Because it is active, the teaching of writing is inseparably a part of the teaching of reading, and the aim of teaching a child to write poetry is not to produce poets, but to produce articulate people, articulateness being the highest form of freedom that society can give to the individual. Mrs. Sloan quotes Kenneth Koch, who should know, as remarking that teaching children to write in this way is not really "teaching," in the limited sense, so much as a matter of allowing them to discover and exploit what they already have.

The author makes clear from the beginning her opposition to what she calls the "skills and drills" approach, which frustrates and stunts all genuine imaginative growth. Emphasis on skills tries to be efficient: It regards learning to read as a largely mechanical operation, to be taught with the least waste of time by repetition of familiar words, adding new words gradually as facility is gained. The argument for such teaching seems extremely plausible, and has only the flaw that the human mind, which always begins as a child's mind, is simply not built that way. Consequently such an approach is not merely immoral and anti-intellectual, it is also miserably inefficient, even in its own terms. Emphasis on drills is, again, an emphasis on a "teaching" process in which the teacher is the active agent, the one who knows, and the students are passive, learning through a mechanism of imitation. That doesn't work either.

I have had no firsthand experience with education below the university level, and while I believe that no theory of criticism is any good at all unless it can be adapted to kindergarten and grade one, I naturally make mistakes when I try to suggest how such an adaptation could proceed. I think most of my mistakes have really been much the same mistake: the mistake of underestimating what a child can respond to. Mrs. Sloan, with more experience, does not make this mistake. She knows that children can respond to tragedy and irony as well as to comedy and romance, and that children want difficulty: If they are practicing jumping over hurdles, they want the highest hurdle they can possibly get over, not a low one that they know they can manage. The author also makes it clear that the notion of there being some danger of distorting "reality" by introducing fantasy and myth to the small child is pure (except that it is very impure) superstition. Such dangers only arise in certain types of bad realism. As C. S. Lewis remarks, no child is going to confuse *Alice in Wonderland* with reality, but a pseudorealistic study about life in a British public school might lead him to expect that school life really was like this. Mrs. Sloan notes that there is now a fashion for realism in children's stories, probably because there is also a fashion for fantasy in adult stories, and adults tend to expect children to make up for their own deficiencies.

When I was about ten I once had to mind the little boy next door, who was about three. He wanted to know what the flowers in the front yard were. I told him they were hydrangeas, and this word, which came out something like "hyainzuz," he repeated all afternoon, chuckling to himself at intervals. Many years later I realized that I had confronted that afternoon one of the primary phenomena of literary education. It is the rare magic word, the mysterious polysyllabic word, that is most likely to become the educational focus, the beckoning light ahead: Similarly, it is the magic story, not the imaginatively squalid story, that is most likely to start the quest for awareness going. Ultimately, everyone exposed to literary education has to try to become a Prospero; otherwise he becomes a Caliban. From the stuttering Dick-and-Jane readers to the foul-mouthed blither of the Watergate transcripts, we realize how many Calibans there are who are quite right in saying:

> You taught me language; and my profit on't
> Is, I know how to curse.

But there are still some Prosperos who have learned how to control the magic of words and make it part of their own experience, and it is to increase their number in society that the present book is devoted.

NORTHROP FRYE
1912–1991

Preface

When the first edition of *The Child as Critic* was published in 1975, its basic premise, that literature belongs at the center of a viable program to develop literacy, was a revolutionary notion. In 1984, the year of the second edition, this was no longer a radical idea, although it was still a novel one. At the beginning of the 1990s, it is a premise that educators have begun to accept. The number of literature-based literacy programs in elementary and middle schools is growing.

While the primacy of literature in the development of literacy is no longer a novel idea, there is still a long way to go before we can say that literature is in place everywhere as the vehicle for helping young children develop ability as readers and writers. Furthermore, the question of *how* it is put in place is as much a concern as that it should be.

The third edition of *The Child as Critic*, revised in keeping with the current trend in literacy development, offers—as did the first two editions—theory and practice to inform the implementation of literature-based literacy programs. Its content supports the conviction that literature is the best means for developing genuine literacy, which includes both the ability *and* the desire to read and write.

Literacy, not a point to be reached but a development over a lifetime, begins in wide reading, in discovering firsthand the delights and satisfactions to be found in the various forms of literature. Literacy through literature begins with each reader's personal response to a literary work, but it does not end there. It continues with study—critical, reflective consideration of what is read—undertaken through methods and materials appropriate to young students.

Works of literature, like musical compositions, cannot, of course, be directly taught. The study of musical compositions we call music appreciation; the study of literary works is *criticism*. Just how literary criticism may be appropriately and significantly undertaken in elementary and middle schools continues to be a primary concern of *The Child as Critic*.

One important function of criticism, as I see it, is to help students toward a conception of the interrelatedness of literary works. This aspect of criticism, which provides a sense of the unity of all literature, must be undertaken within the framework of a theory of literature that describes this unity. Like the two earlier versions of *The Child as Critic*, the third draws upon the literary theory of Northrop Frye. It argues that the unifying principles of literature, as Frye delineated them, may be understood inductively by the youngest students.

The Child as Critic is based on research, both the author's and that of others. Data collected in classrooms where the language arts and other curriculum areas are taught and learned through literature are cited throughout as illustrations of teaching and learning. Many of the teachers in these classrooms are former students in my graduate classes at Queens College of the City University of New York. I am indebted to all these colleagues and especially to Christine Choka, Kathleen Cunningham, Karen Curran, Ellen Goldfarb, Bernice Levy, Kathryn Lewis, Ann Moynagh, Annette Sanchez, and Jane Watson.

The book is intended for teachers, prospective teachers, librarians, language arts supervisors, designers of curricula, and others interested in the teaching of English in elementary and middle schools.

Readers of the first two editions of *The Child as Critic* will find the third edition unchanged in its focus and philosophy. The text of this edition is new, although it includes, updated and reordered, relevant material from the first two editions.

The nine chapters of the book are arranged in three parts. Part I, "Literature and Literacy," consists of two chapters. Chapter 1, "The Case for Literature," argues for the centrality of literature—reading material that speaks in the unique voice of an author with something to say—in programs to develop literacy. Chapter 2, "Toward Literacy Through Literature," discusses, from a research base, the efficacy of a literature-based approach to literacy and how this approach relates to the movement known as "whole-language" teaching and learning.

Part II, "The Unifying Principles of Literature," contains three chapters. Chapter 3, "On Teaching Literature," provides

theory to inform the teaching of literature. In Chapters 4 and 5,
"Likenesses Unify Literature" and "The Circle of Stories," the
unifying principles of literature are delineated to provide teachers with a deductive framework on which to structure students'
inductive learning.

The four chapters of Part III, "Theory into Practice," contain
specific examples of practices and strategies in literary criticism.
Chapter 6, "Poetry and Literacy," argues for the primacy of poetry
in literacy education and provides direction for bringing children
and poetry together in the classroom. In Chapter 7, "Developing
a Sense of Story," the discussion covers methods and materials
for broadening students' experience with prose literature and
includes specific suggestions for implementing independent—
individualized—reading programs in the classroom. Chapter 8,
"Growing as Critics," offers examples of techniques and activities that move students beyond personal experience and response
toward a sense of the unity of literature and a conception of how
the interrelatedness of literary and other verbal constructs affects
both our imaginative and practical lives. In "The Process of Writing," Chapter 9, writing—and other types of composing—are
presented as aspects of criticism. This chapter details, with examples, procedures useful in helping children compose their own
stories and verse.

The book contains a list of resources in literature and language arts, which includes sources useful in book selection. In
addition to general references, bibliographical information is
provided for the children's literature cited in the text. In citing
works of children's literature, I have used what are for me the
best examples, realizing that older works may be out of print.
However, these excellent old favorites are often available in
libraries or as reissued paperback or other editions.

GLENNA DAVIS SLOAN

PART I

Literature and Literacy

The Case for Literature

I think one thing that we can do is to share with children works
of the imagination–those sounds deepest in the human heart,
often couched in symbol and metaphor. These don't give children packaged answers. They invite children to go within themselves to listen to the sounds of their own hearts.
                                    –Katherine Paterson (1989, pp. 34–35)

A sixth-grade teacher asked the 32 children in her urban classroom to reply yes or no to this question: Outside of school, do
you often read books, newspapers, or magazines? Three-quarters
of the class checked no.

In this electronic age, children are likely to feel no urgent need
to read and write. In the world outside of school, whole days may
pass without the necessity for reading and writing. Televised situation comedies and police shows provide the entertainment once
supplied by comics and series books like Nancy Drew and the
Hardy Boys. Tape recorders answer phones and take messages
with never a word written or read. It is quicker and more conven-
ient to pick up the phone instead of a pen to communicate for
business or pleasure. Reading and writing always required more
exertion than talking and listening. Now that alternatives are
available, why make the effort?

For many children, reading and writing have become activities almost exclusively associated with school. One major study
of fifth graders revealed that reading books occupied less than
1% of the children's free time (Anderson, Hiebert, Scott, &
Wilkinson, 1985). While some of these children may be *illiterate,*
unable to read beyond the most rudimentary level, more of them
are likely to be *aliterate,* able to read but choosing not to.

LITERATURE *IS* A "READING PROGRAM"

Literacy is a state of becoming, not a point to be reached. It has barely begun when children acquire the basics of reading and writing, which in themselves are only passive skills, having to do with being an obedient citizen: able to read traffic signs and fill in the blanks of official forms. Knowing *how* to read—and write—is essential, but not in the long run what is important about literacy. What is important is how the skills are developed and what nourishes their development. The truly literate are not those who know how to read, but those who read: independently, responsively, critically, and because they want to. The first real business of reading instruction is to make children want to read. To do that, we must be as concerned with *what* they read as with *how* they read.

Since literature—unique writings that demonstrate excellence of form and expression—addresses itself principally to the imagination, many educators have difficulty in accepting it as more than a diversion. Confronted with the low scores on standardized reading tests of children who read "below grade level," if at all, they insist that the business of the elementary school is to teach "basic skills." Too often this means a tedious program of skill drills. For children who have already learned to hate reading, there could hardly be a more futile approach.

"Is this all there is to reading?" young students must think, struggling with one more workbook exercise in phonics. If children's school experience convinces them that there is no more to reading—and writing—than ho-hum exercises, it is not surprising that they show little interest in becoming consumers or creators of written words.

Children develop their ability to read and write by reading and writing. But reading and writing require considerable effort, and children will not bother to expend it unless their experience convinces them that written words have significance in their lives.

The conviction that reading and writing are worthwhile may well be the single most important ingredient in any program to develop literacy. The promise of better jobs or higher salaries motivates adults to apply themselves in night-school classes. Children are seldom so practical. Prospects of earning a living or succeeding in college are too remote to influence their effort. The young are notorious hedonists, preferring to expend their energies on activities that offer satisfaction here and now.

Unless printed words make a strong appeal to their emotions and imaginations, children will remain indifferent to reading and writing them. For children, printed words must provide wonder, delight, interest, and pleasure, or they won't bother to read, even though they may have learned the rudiments of reading.

Among the masses of printed material available to readers, the works for which we reserve the term *literature* possess the greatest potential to influence the feelings and the imagination. Born of imagination, the unique literary work influences through a direct, intense appeal to that faculty. At its best, literature is art created in words, where, driven by imagination, language is chosen with artistry and skill to construct stories, poems, and informational material with potential to engross, enchant, and enlighten.

Children will become readers only if their emotions are stirred and their imaginations stretched by what they find on printed pages. One way—a sure way—to make this happen is through genuine literature, works that claim consideration because, having something to say, they use language to greatest effect in saying it.

Nothing is more important or practical in the long run than genuine literature. Nothing should come before it. All efforts to teach reading must begin with it. It is only the art of literature that can successfully counter the drawing power of television. Literature, because it is worth reading, nourishes the desire to read.

Concerned when most of her sixth graders admitted to aliteracy, the teacher who was introduced at the beginning of the chapter began a concerted effort to interest them in reading. She started giving regular "book talks" about novels dealing with growing up, an issue of obvious relevance to young adolescents. An important part of the program was reading aloud tantalizing bits from the novels.

Her choices included such outstanding books as *The Sign of the Beaver* (Speare, 1983), *Bridge to Terabithia* (Paterson, 1977), and *The Cybil War* (Byars, 1981a). Making copies of these and similar books available, she encouraged the students to complete them independently. The only assignment: If you liked the book, tell the rest of the class why and read aloud a favorite episode.

Incredibly, some of these children had never before read an entire book. The program resulted in dramatically altered attitude and behavior where reading was concerned. Finally convinced that reading books could be a satisfying activity, all children read at least three; several read many more (Moynagh, 1986).

Another teacher in one of my classes at Queens College, responding to negative comments on an attitude survey administered to fourth graders (over 75% of the class said they'd just as soon do chores in their spare time as read), began to read aloud a series of novels (Curran, 1987). For these resistant readers, she chose relatively short, humorous stories—humor because of its sure appeal for this, or any, age, and short so as not to intimidate them. (In their surveys, many of her students had complained that reading was "difficult" and a "waste of time.") Her choices included *The Blossoms and the Green Phantom* (Byars, 1987), *Anastasia Has the Answers* (Lowry, 1986), *Konrad* (Nostlinger, 1977), and *Lizard Music* (Pinkwater, 1976). Within a month, the children were searching the library for more funny stories, reading them on their own, and recommending them to classmates.

LIMITATIONS OF BASAL READING PROGRAMS

Literature is far and away the most effective "reading program" ever devised. Unfortunately, it has not been the one most widely used in the United States.

Pervasiveness of Basal Readers

For several decades most children across this nation have been taught to read, from kindergarten through eighth grade, exclusively with basal reading programs. These programs are based on the premise that learning to read consists of mastery of a sequential series of skills, best presented through material in which syntax is simplified and vocabulary controlled.

Complete packages of teaching materials, these systems provide the scope and sequence of an entire reading curriculum. They include graded anthologies of selections in children's "readers," instructional strategies detailed in teacher's manuals, practice exercises in workbooks, as well as supplementary material: tests, management systems, visual aids like word and sentence cards, audio tapes, film strips, games, and phonics and skill development charts. The trappings of a basal reading system, besides taking up considerable space on classroom shelves, are major items in school budgets.

Now that illiteracy—and aliteracy—are recognized as serious problems, many educators have begun to question the efficacy of basal systems. They are questioning systems that insist that *how* children read is always more important than *what* they read. They are questioning lock-step skill and drill exercises as the way to develop genuine literacy.

In light of new research in language learning (Harste, Woodward, & Burke, 1984; Smith, 1983), can we continue to accept the idea that reading involves sequential mastery of dozens of separate and distinct skills and abilities? Does it make sense to control vocabulary when, after all, word sense develops through encounters with unfamiliar words, not suppression of them? Children are thrilled by the sight and sound of polysyllabic wonders. Aware of this, Beatrix Potter used five-dollar words like *alacrity* in her nursery tales (Potter, 1912).

Yet, basal reading systems are so entrenched as the methods and materials used across America in reading instruction that objective evaluation of them is rare. They, together with the standardized reading tests that complement them, are so much a part of school culture that it seems difficult for everyone—supporters and detractors alike—to imagine school without them. The Commission on Reading (Anderson et al., 1985), advocating their use while acknowledging their limitations, does not seriously consider alternatives to the basal.

Literature as an Alternative to Basal Readers

An alternative does exist, however, in literature-based literacy programs. Learning to read trade-book literature, a growing body of research informs us, is another way—and a highly effective one in terms of motivation and improved performance—to learn to read (Eldredge & Butterfield, 1986). The exclusive use of basal systems has not and will not lead children toward genuine literacy, which includes both the ability and the desire to read. Learning the basic skill of decoding is essential, of course, but as soon as children can read, they must read real texts. So-called skill building can, and often does, become an end in itself. Readers, workbooks, and audio-visual kits of reading exercises are only skill builders. They are not actual reading material, any more than scales are musical compositions. Participation in a reading program that does not go beyond drills of skills is like learning to play the piano by practicing scales without ever playing a piece of music.

To those who would prescribe increased doses of drills as the cure for illiteracy and aliteracy, advocates for literature respond that even the slowest learner will profit more from the injections for the imagination that literature provides. The capacity of children to experience and enjoy stories, poems, and informational books is not dependent on their ability to decode or read fluently. Like the telegraph operator, they are able to "read" what they hear. Although being read to is not reading for oneself, if what one hears is worth listening to, the desire to read is sure to follow.

Interest in the exploits of storybook characters like Curious George, Madeline, Henry Huggins, Deenie, George and Martha, Encyclopedia Brown, Pippi Longstocking, and Frog and Toad keeps children listening or turning the pages of books. Learning about the eccentricities of long and short vowel sounds does not. Nor do reading snippets of trivia written in flat-footed prose and answering reams of questions on its content. Too much emphasis on skill and drill, far from turning children into readers, turns them against trying to read. From the beginning, they must experience printed words at their best, in continuous texts with the power to involve and engross them.

"Basalization" of Literature

Responding to criticism that the selections in basal readers were bland, trivial, and lacking in literary quality, publishers in recent years have moved to include "literature" in their basal readers. The result, however, is often a "basalization" of an author's text to fit the readability, vocabulary, and sequential skill requirements of the reading system. When unabridged literary works are included, they are typically treated—in the teacher's manual— like any other textbook selections. In most cases, works are shortened, simplified, or rewritten with changed vocabulary, shortened sentences, and modified story lines.

As an example, here are the original first two paragraphs of the tale, "Two of Everything" (Ritchie, 1949).

> Mr. and Mrs. Hak-Tak were rather old and rather poor. They had a small house in a village among the mountains and a tiny patch of green land on the mountain side. Here they grew the vegetables that were all they had to live on, and when it was a good season and they did not need to eat up everything as soon as

it was grown, Mr. Hak-Tak took what they could spare in a basket to the next village, which was a little larger than theirs, and sold it for as much as he could get, and bought some oil for their lamp, and fresh seeds, and every now and then, but not often, a piece of cotton stuff to make new coats and trousers for himself and his wife. You can imagine that they did not often get the chance to eat meat.

Now one day it happened when Mr. Hak-Tak was digging in his precious patch, he unearthed a big brass pot. He thought it strange that it should have been there for so long without his having come across it before, and he was disappointed to find that it was empty; still, he thought they would find some use for it, so when he was ready to go back to the house in the evening, he decided to take it with him. It was very big and heavy, and in his struggles to get his arms around it and raise it to a good position for carrying, his purse, which he always took with him in his belt, fell to the ground, and to be quite sure he had it safe, he put it inside the pot and so staggered home with his load. (pp. 142–143)

The following is the beginning of a version of the same story that appears in *Jumping Up*, a reader in the Lippincott Basic Reading series (Walcutt & McCracken, 1981):

One day Mr. Hak-Tak found a big brass pot. He was sure there must be some use for it. Mr. Hak-Tak decided to take the pot home with him.

As he was going along, his wallet fell to the ground. To make sure he did not lose it, he placed his wallet inside the big brass pot. (p. 150)

In the ruthlessly abridged basal reader version, nothing whatever remains of the leisurely charm and folktale flavor of the original. All detail that establishes who the Hak-Taks are and where and how they live is omitted. The style of the original is lost, leaving readers with a mere summary of the story in language that utterly lacks the storyteller's rhythmic, conversational style.

If well-told tales and carefully crafted poems are not children's reading material in school from the beginning, why should we be surprised that children refuse to read? Where is the motivational power in the thuds and thumps of graceless textbook prose? When it comes to charm, inventiveness, freshness of approach, and imaginativeness, there is no contest between literary language of distinction and language fabricated to serve the questionable purposes of a reading scheme.

LITERACY BEGINS IN LOVE OF LANGUAGE

In the introduction to *The Acts of King Arthur and His Noble Knights*, John Steinbeck (1976) writes:

> Some people there are, who being grown, forget the horrible task of learning to read. It is perhaps the greatest single effort that the human undertakes, and he must do it as a child. . . . For a thousand thousand years humans have existed and they have only learned this trick—this magic—in the final ten thousand of the thousand thousand. . . . I remember that words—written or printed—were devils, and books, because they gave me pain, were my enemies. Then one day, an aunt gave me a book. . . . I stared at the black print with hatred, and then, gradually the pages opened and let me in. The magic happened. (p. xi)

The book his aunt gave Steinbeck was a cut version of the Caxton *Morte D'Arthur* of Thomas Mallory. Steinbeck continues:

> I loved the old spelling of the words and the words no longer used. Perhaps a passionate love of the English language opened to me from this one book. . . . The very strangeness of the language dyd me enchante, and vaulted me into a ancient scene. (p. xii)

A similar story is likely to be found in the biography of every writer. Poets, columnists, and novelists all acknowledge the role of reading in making them writers. Early acquaintance with favorite books instilled in them a passionate love for words. These are the truly literate, who know from experience the power of written words, because these have made a difference in their lives.

The emotional impact of hearing or reading a fine piece of writing can be profound. It may well be the goose-bump experience that leads a child to a lifetime love of carefully crafted language. At the age of seven, Henry James, hiding under a table to hear a chapter of *David Copperfield* read by a relative, was discovered and sent to bed when he burst into tears at the cruelty of the Murdstones. Novelist Walker Percy remembers his father reading *The Jungle Book* and *Treasure Island* aloud to him: "To this day I remember certain passages from Kipling and every concrete detail of the way he read them" (Tyler, 1977, p. 17).

Donald Barthelme has a vivid recollection of being read to as a child, one book in particular whose title he can't recall: "I've been searching for that book all my life. The feeling of it, the tone, I remember: the music, but not the words" (Tyler, 1977, p. 16). Those familiar with the cadences of Dylan Thomas' poetry will not be surprised to learn that his father, a teacher, read him Shakespeare and only Shakespeare from the time he was a toddler.

John Updike (1975), master writer in several literary forms and frequent contributor to the prestigious pages of *The New Yorker*, recalls: "When I was thirteen, a magazine came into the house, *The New Yorker*, by name, and I loved that magazine so much I concentrated all my wishing into an effort to make myself small and inky and intense enough to' be received into its pages" (p. 37).

Poet Eve Merriam acknowledges that certain favorite poems, like the parodies of Mother Goose by Guy Wetmore Carryl and his brother Charles, directly influenced both the style and content of her own writing (Sloan, 1981). Robert Cormier (1986), speaking of his discovery at the age of 13 of *The Web and the Rock*, writes: "I found in Wolfe . . . the tumultuous language that shook my senses, the theme that excited my soul. . . . I knew when I finished that novel the inevitable course my life would take. I would be a writer. No other life would be possible for me."

Andrew Wilkinson, in *The Foundations of Language* (1971), comments: "Many people do not feel a need to develop their language, and the reason is that they are unaware of the possibilities of language. They imperfectly appreciate the nature, the uses, the joy of language" (p. 139). Through encounters with genuine literature—art in words—children can begin to learn about "the nature, the uses, the joy of language."

Literacy begins in hearts, not heads. For some it may begin in the moment of silent awe that follows the reading of a poem like "The Ballad of the Harp-Weaver," by Edna St. Vincent Millay (1924). For others it might start with laughter at the mishaps of Pooh and Piglet or in tears at Charlotte's death. For little ones, chanting the refrain of *Millions of Cats* (Gág, 1928) might be all it takes. There is a story or poem to raise a goose bump on the toughest skin, and we are well advised to help each child find it. A child who has never thrilled to words will remain indifferent to reading and writing them.

LITERATURE EDUCATES THE IMAGINATION

If literature is essential to the development of readers and writers who are genuinely literate, it is also essential to the education of the child's imagination. There is no single definition of imagination. We have no standardized tests to measure it, but this does not mean that its education can be neglected. We know that this creative and constructive power is not exclusive to the artist or inventor. Nor is imagination secondary to intellect or emotions; it is the very core of them. It is through the imagination that we participate in every aspect of our daily lives: in conversation, in relating to others with sympathy and consideration, in making choices and decisions, in analyzing news reports and the speeches of politicians, in evaluating advertisements and entertainment.

Why can literature and the study of it educate the imagination? One reason is that literature itself is born of imagination. The imaginative writer constructs a world that is but never was; within each world there is room for endless imaginative possibilities. A story is not real life; anything can happen; anything goes. Literature illustrates what it is essential for humans to realize: there are no limits for the imagination. Literature makes carpets fly and rabbits talk; it overcomes the tyranny of time and conquers death itself. A Yellow Brick Road leading to an Emerald City will never be found on a road map, but it exists, along with other literary locations and their inhabitants, as an imaginative reality.

Literature, furthermore, has the capacity to develop our imaginative perspective on reality. What we call reality is a confusing tangle of experience: Radios blare at us, advertisers bombard us, we are harassed and hurried, torn in a dozen directions. We have all had the desire, when the confusion of life is at its height, to "get away from it all," "to sort things out," "to see where we are," "to get ourselves together." We feel a need for perspective on our fragmented experience. One way to get it is through literature, the art that describes what happens to human beings as they try to come to terms with living. Literature gives shape to shifting human experience.

Another property of literature worthy of the name is its ability to call forth, as we experience a work, our own imaginative experience, something we "have always known" but couldn't express until a poem, play, or story put it into words and images for us. Thus literature puts us in touch with our own imaginative powers. Nothing is more important for creating a truly human world than realizing the power of the imagination. William Blake said that nothing is real beyond the imaginative patterns we make of reality. Imagination, in Blake's sense, creates reality. In the real world there can be no change or reform of any kind unless we first use our imaginations to describe what sort of life we want to lead, what kind of world we want to live in. The experiencing of a variety of literary works and the appropriate study of them can lead gradually to the transferring of the imaginative habit of mind that literature embodies.

SOCIAL VALUE OF THE STUDY OF LITERATURE

A culture's beliefs and actions take shape around a social vision constructed by the imagination. It is in literary works, particularly myths, legends, and folktales, that these informing social myths are expressed most clearly. Much of the mythology of the United States reflects ideals of self-reliance, independence, industry, tolerance, and respect for democratic process. Mythical figures such as the explorer, the pioneer, and the cowboy embody these ideals, Through encounters with our earliest stories, understanding of subsequent developments in history, politics. religion, and social life is deepened and clarified. Attention to the traditional and classical stories of a culture provides a kind of key to its history. They are more than "just stories." But because they are stories— imaginative constructs—it is possible to examine them with a certain detachment and discover things about our beliefs and actions as a society that we could never learn in any other way.

Every use of words, from the advertisement to the politician's speech, is a verbal structure, just as a literary work is a verbal structure. The same myths—imaginative verbal structures— inform both uses of words. Those who wish to influence others, for good or evil, make use of the same myths we find in literature: pastoral myths, hero myths, quest myths, sacrificial myths. The politician promises to take us back "to the good old days." The advertiser lures us with a description of a holiday retreat "away from it all," or promises to make rugged achievers out of those who eat the right breakfast food. Students who have encountered the genuine form of the myth in literature will be less likely to fall prey to its perverted form in the advertisement. They will know that an advertisement showing the plain, unpopular girl suddenly made beautiful and popular by the use of the right face cream is

nothing more than a version of the Cinderella story. They will recognize that an advertisement showing idealized young men and
women drinking a certain brand of cola while they frolic joyfully
in a summer setting has stolen its conventions from the romance,
a literary form given more to fantasy than to realism.

Such use of language and myth is part of a pervasive social
mythology whose purpose is to persuade us to accept—usually
for another's gain—the standards and values of the society in
which we live. It provides a means of making us adjust to things
as they are or as a profiteer would have us believe them to be.
Some adjustment to society is necessary, of course. But it is important to guard against too much passive acquiescence. Children
especially need a means to fight the effects of the propaganda and
social conditioning of advertising and popular entertainment.

Literacy is a cumulative development over a lifetime. Becoming literate involves more than reading at a rudimentary level. It
embodies some conception of how the imagination works in
creating verbal constructs and how these constructs, literary and
subliterary—advertisements, political speeches, formulaic fiction,
pop songs, and the like—not only share the same elements but
also come from the same roots. Raised on genuine literature, the
truly literate will recognize, in the speeches of politicians, in
popular books and television sitcoms, in pop songs and advertisements, perversions of quest myths, hero myths, and pastoral
myths.

The structures of literature are self-contained; the reality they
present is an imaginative reality. Contemplating these structures
critically and reflectively can help us to develop the capacity to
view with detachment other verbal structures that surround us.
A well-developed imagination, educated on literature, is protec-
tion against social mythology in all its forms: entertainment,
advertising, propaganda, the language of cliché and stereotype,
the abstractions of jargon and gobbledegook. In an irrational
world the trained reason is important, but an educated imagination is fundamental to the survival of a sane society.

2

Toward Literacy Through Literature

Actual stories are the kind of reading that I think most familiar-
izes children with written language. These can range from the
contemporary material found in newspapers and magazines . . .
to the traditional content of fairy tales and adventure stories, to
history and myth. These traditional stories fascinate children—
possibly fulfilling some of their deepest needs (Bettelheim,
1976)—without pandering to an alleged inability to handle complex language or ideas. . . . Indeed, it is through exposure to such
meaningful complexity that children are able to develop and test
their hypotheses about the nature of spoken or written language.
—Frank Smith (1983, p. 48)

For whatever misguided reasons, courses in children's literature—where knowledge about *what* is available for children to
read is provided—are not considered essential for teacher certifi-
cation in New York State. Only courses in so-called basic reading skills—the *how* of reading—are required. Despite this, teachers enroll each semester for our graduate course in children's
literature at Queens College,

They want to learn about children's literature primarily because they see it in terms of its usefulness: The right books can
supply children with the sociological and psychological insights
they need to interpret the world and survive in it; certain books
are valuable as supplemental learning aids in social studies and
science curricula; literature entertains and has potential for moti-
vating children to read. However, at the beginning of the course,

talk of actually teaching literature is likely to draw blank looks
and the occasional objection. Like their supervisors and administrators, most teachers regard the teaching of "basic reading skills"
as the proper major concern of the elementary school. For the
most part familiar only with the behaviorist-psychology approach
to reading instruction, and believers in its sacred books—the basal
reader with its manual—too many educators are convinced that
reading "real" books has nothing to do with teaching the basics
of beginning reading.

"How will we find time to teach literature," teachers ask,
"when we have to teach reading?" The answer: *Use literature
effectively to develop literacy, and you are teaching reading.*

Studies show that the narrative structure of well-written stories "teaches" children to read, that learning to read literature is—
or can be—learning to read. What children read does matter. Important lessons about reading, notably through narrative
structure and convention, are taught by the material read, and it
need not be simplified to the point of inanity, as researchers have
discovered (Bennett, 1979; Fox, 1985; Meek, 1982; Wells, 1982).

Published articles and books about the teaching of reading
to elementary and middle school children number in the hun-
dreds of thousands. However, in this flood of words there is little
agreement on the ways and means best suited to teaching reading. We revere research, but even when we sift through the mul-
titudinous studies looking for those of significance, they do not
provide us with definitive methodology. We soon discover that
reading means different things to different people.

There exists in the field of literacy education a difference in
world view not unlike C. P. Snow's "two cultures," the phrase he
coined to refer to a polarity in mental attitude between the sci-
ences and the humanities (1959). These different perspectives,
for the most part, are representative of two distinct points of view,
which psycholinguist Frank Smith (1983) has characterized as
outside-in and inside-out.

LEARNING TO READ:
OUTSIDE-IN OR INSIDE-OUT

The stimulus-response perspective of the behaviorist psychologist, which has dominated reading instruction for decades, views
reading as separate from other aspects of language development.

This "outside-in" viewpoint focuses on programmatic technology, exemplified by the basal reader and the standardized test. It insists that reading is learned by following a rigid sequential program of skill development. To serve this program, reading material must be simplified by "controlling" vocabulary and sentence structure. Control extends to teachers and pupils, who are led lock-step through texts and workbooks.

Central to the approach is teaching and testing on lettersound relationships, isolated words, and fragmented texts. Fragmentation is a key word of the process. The complex task of reading is split up into discrete segments—ideal, it should be noted, for quantitative testing.

A different perspective is offered by psycholinguistics, a relatively new discipline of the 1960s, which combines the disciplines of linguistics and psychology. The new discipline was established mainly on the theory and research of Noam Chomsky (1957) and George A. Miller (1962), challengers of behaviorist views of language development, in particular those of B. F. Skinner (1957).

Psycholinguists see reading as but one aspect of general language development. The "inside-out" viewpoint is exemplified in the holistic approach to all language development, of which reading is an integral part. It deplores the behaviorist point of view with its initial emphasis on isolated skills, sounds, letters, and lists of words. The psycholinguistic emphasis from the beginning is on helping children to extract meaning from complete texts, to consider the whole before the part. Psycholinguistic theory insists that learning to read can proceed as simply and naturally as learning to speak, when the constraints of testing are lifted and learners are freed to make sense of authentic texts that they find relevant and interesting (Harste, Woodward, & Burke, 1984; Meek, 1982).

In opposition to the behaviorists, psycholinguists emphasize that language is not learned in bits and pieces along a continuum; rather, it develops wholistically, all aspects interrelating in the development. Since the linguistic approach to reading denies that we process language piecemeal, it does not lend itself well to the relentless, quantitative testing on separate aspects of reading, which the behavioristic approach has made the norm in our schools.

Psycholinguistic research confirms that human language behavior is not learned on a stimulus-response model. Language develops functionally, through use that allows learners to grow using trial and experimentation, all their efforts reinforced and encouraged with positive feedback. Notions of word-perfect reading and spelling are rejected as inhibiting. Guessing is encouraged, just as the infant's early attempts to speak, however far from standard speech, are applauded and fostered. Far from favoring constant testing, with its emphasis on right and wrong answers, psycholinguists speak persuasively against the negative, trivializing effects of constant testing on teaching and learning. A far more liberating form of evaluation is determining through observing what language users are trying to do and what help they need in developing their linguistic skills. As for evaluation, the developmental nature of language ability is more appropriately studied through successive samplings of a child's speaking, reading, and writing as these language uses develop in meaningful contexts, than by tests that deal in right or wrong responses (Goodman, Shannon, Freeman, & Murphy, 1988; Goodman, Y., 1989; Shuy, 1981; Smith, 1986).

The inside-out perspective insists that children learn to read by reading, just as they learn to talk by talking. The child who picks up a familiar book and pretends or attempts to read it is more of a reader than the one who can call out correctly words in a list. Reading is understood as something a reader works at in a quest for meaning, often puzzling out a portion that isn't readily understood. The quest for meaning involves desire: to find out what happens next, to learn more about a fascinating character, to find answers to interesting questions. In this perspective the emphasis is on development of ability through encounters with meaningful language in a supportive environment.

Basals: The Behaviorist Perspective

Report Card on Basal Readers, the report of the National Council of Teachers of English Commission on Reading (Goodman et al., 1988) is both a historical and an evaluative examination of the basal reader phenomenon. A comprehensive study of basals indicates that even the best and most recent are based on the "outside-in" perspective of behavioral psychology, which views language as habitual behavior learned through response to stimuli. The flowcharts in the handbooks accompanying basals reflect notions of reading as the sequential development of a series of skills. The alphabetic nature of written language is emphasized in exercises, which implies that reading is decoding alphabetic symbols into sound by the application of spelling-to-sound correspondence rules. Learning, which is teacher-directed, proceeds lockstep in a prescribed sequence, according to a script of questions and expected answers.

Behaviorists, notably Edward L. Thorndyke, influenced William S. Gray, who in 1919 published "Principles of Method in Teaching Reading, as Derived from Scientific Investigation" (Seashore, 1919). Educators, enamored of the results of "scientific investigation," looked for ways to make foolproof the process of learning to read. The basal reader, with its sequenced, fragmented approach to reading and accompanied by the teacher's manual—the stimulus that could exact the correct response from teachers (and ultimately from students)—was settled on as the once-and-for-all answer to reading instruction. For more than 60 years the supremacy of the basal reader, on the surface changing with the times but at bottom still based on old behaviorist theories, has largely gone unchallenged.

Generally, the entrenched methodology exemplified in basal reader systems emphasizes phonics, either implicit (the sound associated with a letter is never pronounced in isolation) or explicit (the sounds associated with letters are identified in isolation and blended to form words). While most experts advocate some use of phonics in teaching reading, they agree that teaching letter-sound relationships apart from actual reading of text is of little value. Filling workbook sheets with phonic abstractions is unprofitable. Instead, readers need to be taught to rely more on syntactic and semantic clues—the context—in their efforts to make sense of text.

Criticisms from Psycholinguistics

Stressing meaning as primary in reading, psycholinguists charge that the basal reader emphasis on word study, which includes heavy doses of phonics, distracts the reader from using syntactical and other clues to meaning imbedded in the language itself. Standing alone, most words are meaningless; they derive meaning from their contexts. Language by its very nature is predictable. Predictability is inherent in the conventional structures in which language is used. Stories, for example, follow predictable patterns; the quest is a typical one. Predictability is built into poetic forms through repetition and rhyme (Goodman, K., 1968; Smith, 1978).

In actual practice, language is learned not from part to whole but from whole to part, through use, in response to a learner's felt need (Halliday, 1975). Spoken language develops in actual social situations, through trial and error, experimentation, and with the help of feedback. *Learning to read and write can and should proceed the same way.*

Yet here we employ a double standard. Any early attempts of a child to speak are applauded, no matter how far these productions stray from standard or adult speech. However, when a child begins formal literacy instruction, it is common for teachers and parents alike to demand nothing less than word-perfect reading and standard spelling.

In learning to read—and write—there needs to be freedom to make mistakes and learn from them. Miscue analysis research (Goodman, Watson, & Burke, 1987) shows that even the so-called "errors" readers make as they read are indications of an active effort to discover meaning. As an example, when the child reads "with a weight of black hair," for "with a wealth of black hair," there is evidence that the text is being interpreted, not merely misread. Furthermore, given the opportunity, readers frequently correct their own miscues in the process of considering the text as a whole.

Basal reader systems, built around control, leave little room for trial and learning through taking risks. The goals for their readers are accurate calling of each word in the text and ability to give prescribed answers to questions on bits and pieces of text.

> The whole justification for an all-inclusive and carefully sequenced basal reader series depends on controlling passive learners. . . . Nowhere in the basals are learners encouraged to decide what is for themselves a good story or text. There is little choice, little self-control, little sense of ownership of their own learning and their own reading. That's not just bad for reading development. It's also bad for their development as thinkers, as learners, as participants in a democratic society. (Goodman et al., 1988, pp. 125, 129)

THE WHOLISTIC APPROACH TO LITERACY

Across the United States and in Canada, New Zealand, and Australia have grown up, from grass roots, groups of Teachers

Applying Whole Language (TAWL). Alliances within this movement informally provide, through conferences and newsletters, support and resources for teachers who believe that all language learning—speaking, reading, and writing—should be fully integrated and child-centered. That is to say, teaching and learning of language need to grow naturally from the actual experience of each specific group of children. Reading, listening, speaking, and writing develop together functionally, in actual situations. Pre-packaged materials like basal reader systems—where language functions are considered as separate entities and activities, ordered and prescribed—cannot be tailored to the needs of a particular group of individuals and therefore are not welcome in whole language classrooms.

Increasingly, "whole language" is regarded, on the basis of research, as the most valid approach to literacy development. However, in the United States, it is far from establishing itself in place of the basal reader. In many of the so-called literature-based, whole-language programs I have observed, the basal reader approach persists; the reading material may be more literary, but the methodology reflects the ingrained thinking that results from years of basal brainwashing.

Frank Smith (1986) attempts to explain why new theories of language, though informed by research, have not been widely translated into classroom practice.

> The view of language and learning that psycholinguists promised was superficially examined by the educational planners and set aside as too vague. Notions that children learned best by being immersed in everyday experience did not fit well with the philosophy that believed in quality control and the delivery of instruction to children as if they were on a production line. (p. 26)

There are other reasons, of course. Supplying basal readers is big business, and their publishers are willing to make superficial changes in their products in a hard-sell attempt—too often successful—to convince the unwary that their methodology is based on the latest research. Furthermore, funds are typically allocated on the basis of need, invariably proven by test results. The basal reader instructional program, which presents reading as a series of discrete, simple steps, translates well into the format of the standardized test. Until alternative ways of assessing reading ability are accepted, the tyranny of the test will prevent whole-language teaching and learning from coming into their own.

Whole-language teaching and learning place emphasis on constructing meaning from authentic texts in the belief that literacy develops from whole to part in a setting that allows for trial and error as language is used purposefully. A whole-language literacy program is literature-based. It features genuine reading material, whether literary or subliterary: children's trade books, both factual and fictional; poetry; periodicals; newspapers; television guides; catalogues; songs; advertisements; even signs and the labels on products.

Implementing Whole-Language Principles

Educators in Australia and New Zealand have for 25 years built successful literacy programs based on psycholinguistic (whole-language) principles (Clay, 1980; Guthrie, 1981). It should be noted that New Zealand, even with an influx of non-English speaking immigrants from the Pacific Islands and Vietnam, has one of the highest literacy rates in the world.

In *The Foundations of Literacy,* Don Holdaway (1979) describes how children in Australia and New Zealand are taught to read not with the primers of a basal reader system but with prose and verse from children's literature. Nursery tales and rhymes, their language made predictable through repetitive patterns, rhyme, and rhythm, supply naturally the repetition of words and phrases considered necessary for success in beginning reading. Furthermore, these authentic stories and verses provide readers with the predictable structures psycholinguists insist are essential for learning to comprehend written language (Stein & Trabasso, 1982).

The developmental program to foster literacy, as described by Holdaway (1984), places literature at its center. Stories and poetry are the reading material; discussing, writing, dramatizing, drawing, listening, reading, and retelling are among the responses to it.

> Over the weeks the children's responses to these opportunities for reflection, discovery and clarification become more and more sophisticated. They always bring to the surface the compelling necessity for sense and meaning. They concede the usefulness of predictable structures of rhyme and rhythm. . . . Aspects of story pattern and new linguistic structures are intro-

duced in memorable and generative ways. . . . Children are
likely to attempt a story of their own following this sort of structure. (p. 52)

Planning and implementing a whole-language literacy-devel-
opment program for a specific group of youngsters, without
teachers' guides and all the other paraphernalia of basal systems,
understandably present a formidable challenge to many teachers. Meeting the challenge, as converts to whole-language teaching testify, results in renewed enthusiasm for teaching (Henke,
1988). Freed by knowledge of how children actually become
literate, these professionals discover in themselves remarkable
resources of creativity and inventiveness as they design literacy
programs tailored for their own students. A major goal of this text
is to support teachers as professional experts, able to operate
independently of systems and schemes created by others.

But what of control, ask the teachers and administrators from
outside-in? How are skills taught? How are records kept? How
do you evaluate? How do you organize?

Characteristics of the Whole-Language Classroom

Perhaps the best way to find answers to these questions is to
watch successful whole-language classrooms in action. Detractors object that a child-centered curriculum leads inevitably to
chaos. This is nonsense. I have observed in whole-language settings for years; what I have seen were organized, creative teachers helping children to be responsible for their own learning and
their use of time—in short, to be active learners.

The following are some of the characteristics of the classes
where I have observed as one particularly interested in literature-
based literacy development.

• Teachers and children meet together daily to plan activities for morning and afternoon sessions. Children articulate their
own goals based on needs and interests; classroom resources and
facilities (e.g., learning centers) are shared on a rotating basis.

• Good books and other reading material are readily available. Although directed reading lessons may also take place, time
is allotted daily for classroom reading of self-selected books for
pleasure and information. Teachers conference regularly with

children about their reading and writing, keeping anecdotal records on children's progress. Skills practice is based on the actual need of individual students, as perceived by the teacher through observation and as requested by the children themselves. Pairs of children often read together. Small groups of children discuss books each of them has read. Children talk knowledgeably about themselves as readers: "I read too fast." "I used to read one word at a time, but I got over that." "I'm a good reader for my age."

• Teachers read aloud to children of all ages. Both teachers and students give book talks to recommend books they enjoyed. "Teaching" of literature proceeds through an inductive process of discovery by children talking together in small groups. One group of fifth graders was able to describe the conventions of the fable (and subsequently wrote original fables) after reading and hearing a selection of fables from La Fontaine to Thurber.

• Research in informational and reference books is in relation to actual situations. In preparation for an apple-picking expedition, one second grade class researched apple-picking procedures and learned about the varieties of apples they would pick.

• Writing, often growing out of reading, is a process in which groups of children work on projects in a workshop setting, critiquing each other's work, revising, and rewriting. Each member of one eighth-grade class possessed a dog-eared copy of the first paragraphs of the short story on which the students worked for many weeks, laboring to get this all-important part of the short story "right." From their extensive study of the short story form, they were aware, as one boy told me, that "the first couple of paragraphs are the key to the whole thing."

• "Publications" of children's work are commonly part of classroom or school libraries. In the apple pickers' class, reports of the experience, which took whatever form the writer favored, were presented in apple-shaped booklets. Included were poems, factual accounts, stories, picture essays, and a play.

• For evaluation, children maintain folders of their written work from the beginning through the end of the school year. These are used in self-evaluations and teacher evaluations. Emphasis is not on "right and wrong" but on making progress. Teachers keep anecdotal records of children's progress; their records are the basis of lessons for individuals and groups, which are tailored to the needs of the children.

- There is evidence of cooperative group learning and peer teaching; teachers are not seen as the only source of assistance and information.

- Second-language speakers benefit from peer tutoring and cooperative small-group learning. They are helped toward full, rich literary lives by reading genuine literature, listening to others read it aloud, and hearing it on tape as they follow a printed text.

- Classrooms are filled with evidence of children's productivity as readers and writers:

> Books created by children on such subjects as computers, sports, Martin Luther King, and dollhouses
>
> Bulletin boards filled with magazine and newspaper articles on topics like acid rain and terrorism
>
> Displays of writing in every form, including biography, narrative poetry, fantasy, and realistic fiction
>
> Copies of letters sent to members of Congress
>
> Copies of fan letters to authors
>
> Newspapers and magazines created by students, containing everything from reviews of television shows and movies to parodies of them
>
> Lists of books recommended by children
>
> Diaries and personal journals
>
> Children's own scripts for Readers Theater, prepared from novels they have read (In Readers Theater, a brief play script of a key scene is created by using actual dialogue from the book; see Chapter 9 for an example.)

There is no single blueprint for the whole-language classroom. Each will be different, for it must be designed with the needs and abilities of a particular group of children in mind. Language activities are natural and real, arising out of the actual experiences of the children. Talk centers on a story they have heard. Research grows out of a need to know. No textbooks in language or literature are required, but authentic reading materials are in abundance.

Whole-language teachers serve as guides and facilitators, motivators and mentors. They are open, organized, flexible, involved, interested, and enthusiastic. They know their students well because they listen and observe to ascertain what the students need to help them grow. Whole-language teachers know that education has very little to do with explanation but everything to do with engagement and involvement.

LITERATURE DEVELOPS LANGUAGE ABILITIES: REVIEW OF RESEARCH

Reading rewritten literature in textbooks is not the way children learn to read by reading. Reading authentic literature in its original form is the way. To make this statement is not to present a new idea. For decades, there have been educators who recognized the limitations of basal reading systems in the development of literacy. Shirley Koeller (1981), reviewing 25 years of *The Reading Teacher,* discovered continuous advocacy, supported by the results of research studies, for the use of children's literature in programs to teach reading. Among those who have insisted that literature belongs at the center of any program to develop literacy are Jeanette Veatch (1959), Walter Barbe (1961), Charlotte Huck (1961), Leland Jacobs (1965), and myself (Sloan, 1975, 1984). The impressive results of extensive research support this advocacy.

Dorothy Cohen's (1968) classic study with 580 academically retarded inner-city second graders provided clear evidence that the daily reading aloud of appealing, well-written stories resulted in dramatically increased ability in word recognition and comprehension, as measured by standardized tests, particularly for children with the lowest initial scores.

The Cohen study, replicated by Bernice Cullinan, Angela Jaggar, and Dorothy Strickland (1974) with second graders from low socioeconomic backgrounds in New York City, again demonstrated that the groups who were read to, who became involved with actual books, and who had their own trade books to explore far outstripped in standardized reading test results control groups who used basal readers during the same period.

Nancy Larrick (1987) reports similar successes with 225 kindergarteners in a New York City school where 92% of the children were from non-English speaking homes, 96% were below the poverty level, and 80% spoke no English on entering school in September. The experimental treatment for these children was Open Sesame, a program offering immersion in the best books written for children through daily reading aloud; unpressured, pleasurable opportunities to practice reading from real books; phonics instruction offered only in close conjunction with the reading of actual texts; and dictation by the children of stories—used subsequently as reading material—based on their own experiences. In June, all 225 children were able to read their own dictated stories and simple books. Some read on second-grade level. "Best of all," writes Larrick (1987) "they loved to read stories and were proud to be readers" (p. 189). Follow-up studies indicate that these children continue to do well, 60% of them reading on or above grade level at the end of first grade, and this on tests that stress phonics, not comprehension.

Carol Chomsky (1978) worked with third graders, remedial readers since first grade, who "hated" reading, decoded painfully, but could not read—readers whose progress had come to a standstill. The children listened individually to self-selected tape-recorded stories while following along in the printed text. Gradually, after a month in which they completed up to 20 readings, they achieved fluency and began to transfer their new skills to other material. Comprehension and word knowledge increased by one to two grade levels on subsequent standardized tests. Writing ability improved. Most significant was the change from a negative to a highly positive attitude toward reading and writing.

In an earlier study, Chomsky (1972) had found that reading aloud to children ages 6 to 10 a variety of literary materials at different complexity levels strongly influenced linguistic development at all ages. Prereaders at high linguistic stages heard more books of greater linguistic complexity each week than did prereaders at lower linguistic stages. Far from confusing the prereader and beginning reader, hearing the authentic language of folktales strengthened vocabulary and comprehension. Chomsky comments:

> The written language is potentially of a more complex nature than speech, both in vocabulary and syntax. The child who reads (or listens to) a variety of rich and complex materials benefits from a range of linguistic inputs that is unavailable to the nonliterary child. (p. 23)

Michael Tunnell (1986) describes outstanding success with an individualized reading and writing program with fifth graders.

Children read daily books of their own choosing and heard books read aloud by the teacher. Response to the books was made through a variety of reading and writing activities: sharing books, writing reviews, and developing displays. An effort was made to use actual books in all curriculum areas. Skill practice was based on individual and group need as demonstrated by actual reading and writing. After 7 months, the average gain, as measured by a standardized reading test, was one grade level. Even more important, surveys, administered before and after the treatment, showed dramatic positive change in attitude toward reading.

I obtained pre- and post-treatment data from six inner-city and suburban classrooms where literacy development was partially literature-based (Sloan, 1988). In these classrooms, reading instruction included mandated directed reading from basal readers and other reading systems, skills development, reading of self-selected trade (library) books, and listening to books read aloud. For all cases studied, standardized reading scores measuring comprehension and vocabulary showed an average gain of one-and-a-half grade levels. Examination of pre- and post-treatment writing samples showed growth in syntactical complexity and vocabulary range in 68% of the cases. While these gains may, in part, be attributed to other variables, it is interesting to note that the gains were consistent for all six classes. Constants in these classes were daily sessions of reading aloud by the teacher from fine prose and verse and periods of independent reading from self-selected books with literary and interest value.

Millions of words have been written by educators and researchers about literacy: what it is, how to achieve it, how to measure it. Until the recent, tentative trend toward literature-based reading programs began, the words of advocates for these programs went unheeded. Perhaps we need to hear what children have to say on the subject of reading real books in school. These comments were written by seventh graders who participated with me in a reading program that consisted of reading in class self-selected trade books with no strings of questions attached. Conferences with the teacher and oral reports to the class were all that were required.

> "It was sure different getting to read real books in school."
> "What I like best about special reading [the name given to the program] was getting to pick out what I read."
> "I never knew reading in school could be this fun."

"I read all the books I wanted to because you didn't have to
write a book report after every book."
"Special reading is nothing like regular reading [using a basal
or "skill-building" booklet]; that's the best thing about it."

The last word (for many educators) on the subject: All seventh graders in the special reading program gained one to two
grade levels during the year, as measured by standardized tests
of comprehension and vocabulary. For other equally important
gains—interest, enthusiasm, joy in reading—there were no formal measures, only the children's changed reading behavior and
their own words in praise of "special reading."

PART II

The Unifying Principles of Literature

3

On Teaching Literature

A good story is sufficient unto the day. It is complete as it stands. If it has something to teach, let it teach in its own sufficiency. In other words, let it be.

—Natalie Babbitt (1990, p. 703)

As long as teachers use basal reader systems to teach reading, the procedures to follow—questionable though they may be in terms of what we know about language acquisition—are spelled out for them in comprehensive manuals. For the alternative route, the development of literacy through literature, there is no handy guidebook to follow. What it means "to study literature" remains an open question, particularly in the elementary school, where until recently the actual teaching of literature has never been an issue for serious consideration.

Literature to some extent is included in a peripheral way in most elementary classrooms: It is used to teach reading skills, inculcate moral values, develop positive self-concepts, and the like. Teachers are exhorted in general terms to provide rich literary environments for young students, to encourage them to read widely, to help them to read critically and appreciatively. Excellent college texts exist for courses in children's literature, which include both the rationale and some methodology for promoting meaningful experiences with literature at the elementary level (Cullinan, 1989; Huck, Hepler, & Hickman, 1987). Even taking into account the current movement toward literature-based literacy programs, the fact remains that the actual study of literature is not widespread in elementary schools in the United States, nor has the question of what this study entails at the elementary level been resolved (Walmsley & Walp, 1989).

Little has changed in the 20 years since Norine Odland (1969) reported:

> There is interest in the subject, but there are more questions than answers about objectives, content and approaches for teaching literature in kindergarten through grade six. . . . The expression "teaching literature" is used relatively infrequently . . . . The broader, more general interpretations of literature in the elementary school expand into use of terms such as language, language arts, personal reading, individualized reading, interests and tastes, reading guidance, literature readers, appreciation, and variations of these. (p. 1)

Teachers in my graduate classes often tell me, before our discussion of what it means to teach literature, that significant literary study is beyond the scope of younger students. The proposal to study literature as an art is rejected by many who fear that children's sense of wonder and delight in story and poetry are jeopardized if they are asked to consider their literary experiences as anything more than diversion.

This curious viewpoint suggests that study, like medicine, must be unpleasant to be effective. Even those who believe that the benefits of teaching literature are too important for it to be approached in a haphazard and unsystematic fashion are wary of formalizing the teaching of literature in the elementary school. This unwillingness may be an indictment of their own educational experience in classrooms where the study of poems was an exercise in verse vivisection and the reading of a story signalled the assignment of a page of questions to be answered for homework.

THE NEED FOR THEORY

In order to plan effectively for the literary education of the young, we need to clarify our notions of what it means "to teach" literature. The fundamental concepts on which the study of literature might be based have not been given adequate consideration. The teaching of literature suffers in comparison with science and mathematics from not having more theory of this kind. It should be as possible to educate the imagination systematically through literature as it is to train the reason through science and mathematics. It is as easy, if not easier, for children to grasp basic literary concepts like plot and rhyme as it is for them to understand sets and equivalent fractions.

There is no legitimate excuse for delaying significant instruction until a child comes of high school age. Young children are perfectly capable of genuine intellectual activity if it is tailored to their needs, interests, and level of intellectual and linguistic development. Elementary literary study ought to be progressive and systematic, providing a sound basis for more advanced study.

The study of literature typically begins with the consideration of literary works as separate entities through a variety of critical approaches, most of which focus entirely on the content of the work. Selections may be considered for their sociopolitical, ethical, or psychological significance; or they may be examined as representative of a genre or the writing in a particular historical period. Study of a text may center on stylistic analysis. The possible approaches to a work are many and varied.

Both as a student and a teacher, I found this study of individual works—though often exhilarating and challenging—to be incomplete. Even when works were considered together—by historical period, genres, or other means of categorization—the study lacked something. It brought no sense of what literature as a whole was all about.

It was in the work of Northrop Frye that I found the missing piece in the study of literature. Frye argues and demonstrates that literature is not a miscellaneous pile of discrete works, but an order of words, a coherent structure in which works are related to each other like members of a large, extended family, with a family tree traceable to the earliest times. Further, he shows how all imaginative verbal constructs, whether literary or subliterary (advertisements, television sitcoms, comics, pop songs) are related. An awareness of these relationships brings with it a sense of the significance of literature as the continuous journal of the human imagination, an interrelated body of imaginative verbal structures that examine every aspect of human experience, real or imagined. This awareness brings to the study of literature a sense of its immediate significance in our lives, an understanding that does not come to students who leave school with only vague random impressions of the poems, plays, or novels they studied.

A viable study of literature leads to an understanding of literature as an order of words whose verbal structures relate both to each other and to subliterary verbal structures. To make this happen, study needs to be founded on a theory that delineates the

unifying principles of literature. The delineation of these principles is possible only if literature is seen in terms of structure as
well as content.

Northrop Frye, whose comprehensive literary studies convinced him that literature is mainly structure rather than all
content, was the first to attempt a delineation of the unifying principles of literature. He provided a scheme that allows us to see
literary works as parts of a whole. His literary theory, set out in
its most complete form in *Anatomy of Criticism* (Frye, 1957), provides a framework for systematic literary studies that follow a
deductive pattern.

Frye's vision of the fundamental unity in literature began with
his extensive study of the work of the eighteenth-century poet,
William Blake. He discovered within Blake's symbolic structures
a recurrent pattern—the myth of the world created, fallen, redeemed by divine sacrifice, and moving toward apocalypse and
rebirth. In his study of Blake's symbolism, Frye found evidence
that suggested the existence of archetypes and organizing principles for the whole of Western literature. *The Great Code: The Bible
and Literature* (Frye, 1982) takes its title from Blake's comment
that the Old and New Testaments are the great code of art.

Literature as a whole Frye calls the "one story" of human-
kind. The one story is the quest of the human imagination for
identity. The framework of all literature is a myth or archetypal
story that goes like this: Once people lived in a paradisal garden
or golden age in harmony with nature. They lost their perfect
home, became alienated from nature and each other, and subject to time and death. The metaphorical quest to recover the lost
golden age-identity, wholeness, unity—is the framework of all
literature. This imaginative quest ranges from the height of our
dreams—what we most desire—to the depths of our nightmares—
what we most fear and dread.

In supplying us with a vision of imaginative possibilities, literature contributes to our personal visions of the truly human
and humane society. One of the major purposes for studying
literature is to effect a transfer of its imaginative energy and
vision to the student; in other words, to educate the imagination.
This, of course, cannot take place without a sense of the "big picture" of literature. Specifics of Frye's theory are examined in detail
in Chapters 4 and 5.

While it does not supplant other critical methods, Northrop
Frye's literary theory supplies an umbrella for them. When we

look at literature from his viewpoint, we have a panoramic perspective, lacking in other approaches, that allows us some sense of the unity of all literature.

LITERATURE AS ART

Literature is one of the arts. Any plan for teaching it must recognize and respect this fact. For one thing, this means that literature is not a subject to be learned in any factual sense; indeed, crucial to its study is making the distinction between imaginative verbal structures and passages of discourse like those in an encyclopedia. If this distinction is made, students and teachers are less likely to try to extract literal meaning from literary works, to glean "facts" from poems or "key ideas" from stories.

Literary theorist Louise Rosenblatt (1938, 1978) makes this point by insisting that literature, as art, must first be read aesthetically. Rosenblatt distinguishes two approaches to reading, which she calls aesthetic and efferent. In an aesthetic reading of a work, we pay attention not only to the sense of the words but also to their sound, rhythm, and other literary elements and their emotional effect on us. The aesthetic, "lived-through experience" of a work is different from an efferent (from the Latin, *efferre*, "to carry away") reading of it. In the latter case, the reader purposefully studies the text to extract information or analyze the writer's technique. The same text may be read both aesthetically and efferently; that is, one may first read a poem or novel aesthetically, uncritically experiencing the artwork. Then the same poem or novel might become the subject of a more objective, efferent reading to examine, say, its rhyme scheme or plot development.

What Rosenblatt (1978) calls her "transactional theory of reading" reminds teachers of an obvious fact, too often overlooked in teacher-centered examinations of literary texts, where individuals' responses are set aside in favor of predetermined appropriate responses and "right" answers. That fact is that each reader enters into a transaction with a text in an effort to make it meaningful. Teachers need to keep in mind that no two readers will respond in precisely the same way to a work. Past experience—with literature and in general—prejudices, biases, and the like affect an individual's first (and subsequent) responses to a work.

Rosenblatt's work has important implications for literary study. In considering literature as art—that is, in the reading of stories, poems, and plays—the efferent stance is inappropriate, particularly in connection with a first reading, which ought to center on an aesthetic experiencing of the artwork. During the aesthetic experiencing of a work, readers ought not to be asked to gather information about content or to make summaries, paraphrases, and analyses appropriate to efferent reading. Even in efferent readings, poems and novels are not to be subjected to searches for main ideas or ransacked for factual information. A social studies textbook or a factual article in the newspaper is more suited to this treatment. Students who are asked to explain a poem or novel as though these forms were pieces of information are receiving confusing messages.

More appropriate in a first consideration of an artwork is a request for the reader's or listener's affective response. What feelings did the piece arouse? Did it leave a satisfied sense of completeness or inevitability? Was it believable? Even in connection with later, efferent readings, care must be taken to avoid treating poems and stories as factual or informational pieces. Helping readers to have a clear sense of the intent or purpose of a work is essential.

The uniqueness of each individual's response to a work needs to be encouraged and respected. Response, after all, is not to the text but to what the individual reader has made of the text. However, one should be prepared to return to the text to illustrate how and why it affected feelings and influenced interpretation. Explanations are always better when they include text in their support.

CRITICISM: THE STUDY OF LITERATURE

Since literature is a form of art, it cannot be directly taught like a skill such as swimming or driving a car. Because this is so, we need a way of talking about what we do when we "teach literature." In music, we don't say we "teach musical compositions," but we do say we teach music appreciation. What we teach and learn when we study literature, from kindergarten through graduate school, is criticism.

Criticism begins in the experiencing of literature in all its forms. It begins when young children learn to listen to a story or poem as a whole, delighting in it as an artistic entity. It involves making a distinction between imaginative verbal structures and passages of factual discourse.

Comprehension of story content and form is part of criticism, with emphasis on the affective and imaginative as well as the cognitive aspects of comprehending. The teacher helps pupils master the ability to see stories and poems as imaginative verbal constructs by asking questions specifically designed to foster literary understanding. Such questions focus the child's attention on the elements of story as they interact in the shaping and structuring of the literary work as a whole, not on bits and pieces of content. These are questions that center, for example, not so much on what characters do and when, but on why they have to behave as they do to make the story happen.

The child's response to literature is a central aspect of criticism. The response may come in the form of a question or comment; it may involve sharing a favorite poem or retelling a familiar story; it may be an original composition in words, a drawing, a dramatization, a puppet play, a dance drama, or the story board for a film or a video.

Criticism used in relation to elementary school literary study is considered by some as too big a word. It conjures up pictures of scholars in ivory towers writing articles for learned journals. But criticism as here defined and described is not study that goes beyond the capabilities of younger students, as subsequent chapters will demonstrate.

In any case, children begin to be literary critics even before they can talk, wriggling off a lap if a story doesn't please them or snuggling down to hear it again—and again—if it does. We recognize the mark of a critic on dog-eared copies of old favorites on a toddler's bookshelf and on well-worn picture books in the public library. When older readers can't find the latest Beverly Cleary or Judy Blume on the library shelves, they register their preferences for these books by filling out reserve cards at the librarian's desk. In expressing preferences, children are acting as critics of literature. But there is more to being a critic than knowing what we like.

Growth in criticism is based on knowledge. Experiencing literature is therefore the first step toward becoming a critic of it. However, just as experiencing a city full of buildings is not studying architecture, so experiencing poems and stories is not studying literature. Its study involves a number of things, including both free response and guided response; the objective of the latter is to heighten and illuminate personal experience. It is a systematic study that proceeds from a teacher's deductive framework to an inductive process on the part of students to discover for themselves how the human imagination works as it creates art from words.

Criticism in this sense is not evaluative criticism such as the book reviewer engages in, although evaluation may be a part of it. It involves comprehension of both the content and the form of a work. Further, it is the attempt of students to examine how and where each new work they encounter fits in relation to all the other literature they know. It involves going beyond personal preferences and value judgments toward a conception of literature as an order of words, a coherent structure in which all works, old and new, interconnect with one another. This sense of continuity, of one step leading to another, of details fitting into a larger design, is central to criticism at elementary and all levels of education. Good teachers of literature help children to make sense out of each literary experience and to go on to discover patterns and make significant connections among all of their literary experiences. In addition, they lead students to an awareness of how literary experiences relate to their daily life and to other imaginative verbal structures such as those found in advertising, comics, and popular music. There needs to be created, through criticism, a sense of the progressive and systematic, an awareness of the significance of literature that goes beyond the experiencing of individual works.

Personal Response: The Beginning of Criticism

Children's responses to the literature they encounter are central aspects of criticism. Response is both free and guided, the teacher building upon initial response to guide young critics to a greater insight and appreciation of literary works and literature as a whole.

The lack of a comprehensive theory to inform elementary criticism results in fuzzy thinking about what it means "to teach" literature. When I ask teachers to suggest a plan of study for a novel or poem, they usually pattern their approach on one of two models: the particular style of literary analysis they remember from their own high school and college classes—typically a detailed analysis of content, often from either a psychological or a sociological viewpoint—or the methodology familiar to them from basal reader manuals and the guides to literary works that are proliferating as resources for teaching children's literature-based literacy programs.

The appropriateness of these approaches needs to be considered both in terms of our goals for elementary literature teaching and with acknowledgment that literature, one of the arts, must be studied as art. A major goal of the elementary literature program is to develop fluent, independent readers who turn eagerly to books for enjoyment and information. This goal will never be achieved through the overteaching recommended by many guides and teacher's manuals.

At every level in elementary and middle school there needs to be freedom simply to read. Children learn to read by reading and being read to. As discussed in Chapter 2, a substantial body of research provides evidence that the act of reading as well as the activity of listening to literary language read aloud results not only in improved reading ability but in improvement and development of all language abilities: listening, speaking, and writing (Clarke, 1976; Durkin, 1966; Smith, 1973; Wells, 1986).

For many teachers, "to teach" means "to question." While good questions are effective teaching tools, they can be overused. (Questioning and other techniques in criticism are discussed in Chapters 7 and 8.) In many cases, the reams of teacher-made questions that follow the reading of every book, story, or poem ask readers and listeners for inappropriate responses to the reading of literature. Often these questions are merely superficial examination of trivial details of content; just as often, they improperly—and impossibly— demand translation of the poetic or metaphoric into factual, discursive prose. (What does this poem mean?)

If children are to grow as critics of literature, they must begin with the broadest possible experience of it, often with no strings of questions attached. For young students criticism begins in the experiencing of literature in all its forms and with their personal response to it.

Another goal of literary study is articulateness. Trying to express orally or in a journal one's personal experience of a literary work or attempting to explain what an author did to make a poem or story "work" are exercises in becoming articulate, a skill that—like reading—is developmental, growing with practice and guidance.

Teacher-researchers in my classes discovered that most children at all levels needed encouragement to express their initial responses to stories and poems. The teachers explored ways of eliciting responses without imposing adult viewpoints or giving the children the idea that there is any single or correct initial response to a given story or poem.

Conversation after a reading was found to yield the most spontaneous response, especially if it took place in groups smaller than a whole class. In priming free response, the following questions and comments were found to be most effective:

> You were all listening hard to that story. Why was that? (Alternatively: Some of you seemed not interested in the reading. Why was that?)
> If you could ask the writer questions, what would they be?
> Do you recall having any strong feelings as you listened? Describe them or act them out.
> Did the story leave you feeling satisfied? Did the story leave you with a sense of completeness? Why or why not?
> Would you like to hear the poem (or story) again?
> Why was this a good story (or poem) for you especially?

In conversations with children about their responses to the literature they read and hear, it helps teachers and care givers to have a sense of the level of literary understanding generally typical of children at different stages of development. What follows are generalizations of literary capabilities by age group as developed by students in my graduate classes, after observing and recording the reactions and responses of individuals and groups of children.

Preschool

- Learns through listening; will attend to the reader's voice even when material read is beyond understanding
- Learns what books are and how they are used
- Helps to "read" stories by joining in on repeated words and phrases
- Responds with body movements like pointing, clapping, and talking to the book and its characters
- Follows story sequence through pictures
- Insists on accuracy in retelling and rereading
- Begins to distinguish among different types of books: make-believe, stories about everyday life, books that invite participation

- Becomes selective, preferring some stories, poems, and types of books over others
- Repeats independently words and phrases from books
- Engages in reading-like behavior: holds book, turns pages, "reads" by retelling from memory
- If asked for comments about a book, is likely to tell what happened in it, often focusing on one incident

Primary Grades

- Listens to longer, more complicated stories and books
- Asks more "Why?" questions about characters, pictures, and plots
- Watches cartoons and stories on TV, recognizing stock characters (hunter, hunted) and basic plots (the chase)
- Anticipates what will come next in a story
- Shows need for resolution in stories
- Categorizes stories more precisely
- Re-creates stories and creates original ones through pictures, dramatic play, writing, or dictating
- Repeats jingles and rhymes from books and TV; begins to enjoy puns, riddles, and jokes
- Distinguishes between make-believe world of stories and reality
- Begins to read independently, often choosing what has been read aloud

Middle Grades

- Reads independently and selectively; enjoys stories with dramatic action and conflict or humor
- Knows story genres: folktale, myth, fable, fantasy, realism
- Understands and uses literary terms: character, plot, flashback, suspense, point of view
- Predicts outcomes
- Recognizes recurrent character types: hero, heroine, villain, minor supporting characters
- Distinguishes tone and mood
- Notes similarities among characters in different stories: "This stepmother is a witch!"
- Recognizes the style of particular authors and prefers one over another
- Becomes interested in who makes stories and how; enjoys read-

ing about and meeting authors; favorite question of authors:"
Where do you get your ideas?"

Upper Grades

- Is familiar with patterns of recurring images and their significance: confusion and chaos contrast with peace and serenity,
light and calm with darkness and storm
- Recognizes allusion and metaphor, although often unable to
articulate this knowledge without help; enjoys wordplay; appre-
ciates jokes, puns, and riddles
- In original writing features characters and plots that reflect
viewing and reading
- Resolves own stories more satisfactorily, if only by expedient
means: character in a tight spot wakes up—the adventure was
only a dream; an extraneous character is introduced to "save
the day"
- Associates literary experiences; stories read and heard are compared with those seen on TV or in movies

Value Judgments

Direct experience of literature is highly personal and subjective and likely to result in a value judgment rather than a literary
one. These judgments are generally statements about the immediate effect of a work on the reader or listener. An individual's
personality, past experience, and predilections are reflected in the
first response to a literary work.

Questions to children about what they like and dislike are not
only futile in the critical sense but also likely to be inhibiting.
Refinements of taste, desirable though they may be, result from
prolonged experience with the widest possible variety of art, and
they cannot be taught or caught from another.

Teachers who attempt "to teach good taste" do so at the risk
of alienating young readers who, at a particular time in their lives,
may find Nancy Drew or the Hardy Boys the nonpareil of literary form. In any case, series books serve an important purpose
in developing fluency in reading because of their stock characters, predictable plots and episodes, and simple language.

Personal preference, redeemed by honesty, should, like grief,
be private and respected. Often it is difficult to express in words

beyond "I hated it" or "I loved it." This first response, a value judgment, is only the first step in criticism.

What one likes is often what one has experienced; the new
and unusual are likely to be suspect. Skilled teachers broaden
experience by introducing material the children are not likely to
find on their own, such as the work of more challenging authors
like Lloyd Alexander, Virginia Hamilton, or Katherine Paterson.
Broad experience with a wide variety of reading material of relative merit at all levels of difficulty is the best way to develop personal standards and expand sensibilities.

CONCLUSIONS

For the child as critic, criticism begins in the experience of
literature and in personal response to it. But it does not end there.
It continues with study that aims to unify and integrate all of the
students' literary experiences and lead them to a sense of literature not merely as a collection of unrelated works—some of which
they enjoy and some of which they detest—but an order of words,
an interrelated structure. (This aspect of criticism is considered
in Chapter 8.)

Children, with materials and methods appropriate to their
level of maturity, can make a significant beginning in literary
criticism. As students proceed through the levels of formal education, the basic understandings they acquire in elementary
and middle school will provide a foundation for further study.
Through their consideration of the unifying principles of literature, children will gain a broader conception of what literature
is and how it works.

The aim of literary study at this level is not to develop psuedo-
scholars parroting literary principles. The aim is to develop truly
literate human beings who have internalized some of the imaginative energy and articulateness of literature.

Study worthy of the name takes students, whatever their ages,
beyond the limitations of subjective experience. A growing sense
of the continuity of literature, of one step leading to another,
of details fitting gradually into a larger design, is essential to
criticism.

Emphasizing the exploring part of the mind, teachers help students to discover that literature is even more than books of good

stories and poems or useful information. It is proof, when its art is preserved, of the power of imagination. Indeed, far from being a collection of unrelated works, literature as a whole is the continuous journal of the human imagination. The next two chapters present the unifying principles that are the basis for this comprehensive look at literature.

Good teachers of literature can help children to make sense out of their literary experiences, to see patterns, to make connections, to draw significant, enlightening conclusions, and to relate these experiences to the imaginative verbal structures they encounter in daily life through television, comics, advertising, and popular music. Participating in this effort to express understandings and insights, students necessarily learn to use words with increasing ease and precision. This study—experiencing, responding, reflecting, responding again—has the potential to foster genuine literacy because it is centered in literature, where unique works of art offer proof of the power that words possess when they are apt and ordered with imagination.

4

Likenesses Unify Literature

The order of words is there. . . . The fact that literature is based on unifying principles as schematic as those of music is concealed by many things, most of them psychological blocks, but the unity exists and can be shown and taught to others, including children.

—Northrop Frye (1976b, p. 118)

Without its own conceptual framework to contain and inform it, literary study—criticism—moves outside itself, typically utilizing concepts from other studies in the humanities, like history and philosophy. For example, literary works are frequently considered chronologically, a concept borrowed from history. Another common approach to literary study, which focuses on content, leans toward philosophy; here certain stories, poems, and plays are considered as repositories of moral and social ideals, and study consists mainly of gleaning from them profound axioms of the human situation. These approaches, however valid, provide no sense of the unity and coherence of literature as a whole or insight into what literature is and how it works.

Criticism has to be based in literature itself. A conceptual framework within which study may be systematic and developmental needs to come from organizing principles actually present in literary works. Literature grows out of itself; new works are recognizably related to old, just as a baby is a new and unique individual as well as an example of a human being, a descendant of a long line of other humans. Literature does have a context of its own; the context of each work is its place with regard to other works.

Literary works relate through their likenesses. These likenesses—similarities recurring throughout all literature—are discussed in this and the next chapter; through them literature is unified. Their delineation provides a conceptual scheme that allows us to see each work as a part of a whole.

HOW LITERARY WORKS INTERRELATE

Literature is more than a collection of unrelated poems and stories; the more we read the more obvious this becomes. Hercules and Superman were created centuries apart but they are recognizable as the same character type: the hero with magical powers. We find images like gardens and wastelands in the Old Testament and in the ballads of folksingers. That love is more powerful than any evil or even death itself is a theme of stories as different as the old tale *Beauty and the Beast* and the more recent *Charlotte's Web* (White, 1952). We recognize the shape of the romance story—the adventurous quest—in ancient epics, westerns, space odysseys, and the countless cops and robbers shows of television. In the latter, a crusading attorney or police officer, like the dragon-slaying knight of old, sets out to confront and capture modern-day dragons who may appear in the shape of corrupt politicians, drug dealers, murderers, or child molesters.

Archetypes

In literature, as well as in other verbal structures such as advertisements, certain elements and structural patterns are recurrent; this is evident in works both old and new, classical and pop. These patterns or models—fundamental and ancient—recur often enough to be recognizable as aspects of all literary experience; as such, they are archetypal.

Archetypes can be characters (wise old men or women); events (rites of initiation); symbols (innocence equated with youth); plots (the Cinderella story, the quest); themes (love is more powerful than evil); images (wastelands and gardens); motifs (transformations, patterns of three). Archetypes are repeated patterns that recur in the literature of every age. They are found in the Bible, in mythology, in folk literature. Nor are these units of imaginative thought common only to the main body of literature; they turn up in comics, films, song lyrics, and children's drawings. Archetypes are forms of imaginative thought, present in both primitive and sophisticated art. These repeatable units of imaginative experience occur constantly and unpredictably. Their existence makes it possible to connect one literary work with another.

Convention and Genre

The word *convention* expresses another kind of similarity found in literature. If we read a detective story, for instance, we expect to find certain elements in it—a crime, someone to solve it, a criminal who is apprehended. Each detective story, like each game of chess or checkers, is different enough from others to make it a distinct experience, yet similar enough to make us recognize it as one of a type.

In addition, we find that literary works fall into categories or genres. Most of these genres or forms have long histories. Primitive rituals and dances, for example, are known to be the antecedents of drama.

The primary literary categories are drama, prose fiction, lyrics, epics, and nonfiction forms like the essay and autobiography. Genres may change over time; new forms may evolve. However, literature derives its forms from itself, and every form may be traced back to the earliest times. *Huckleberry Finn* and *Moby Dick* are epics of a new country, the United States, but even so they have elements in common with the *Iliad* and the *Odyssey*, epics of ancient Greece—among them disguises, clever lies to ensure survival, and the idea that human friendships can be stronger than disaster. It is a fact that writers write out of their experience with literature, no matter how innovative we may consider their new works to be.

LITERARY PATTERNS FROM MYTHOLOGY

From its beginnings, literature has been people's imaginative attempt to give shape, order, and structure to their experience. Literature's roots are with myth and ritual, myth being the spoken part of a ritual, the story that the ritual enacts. Early religious rituals aimed at securing the well-being of a group of people, and most shared the same general pattern: They depicted the death and resurrection of a god-king in a series of episodes that typically included a battle in which the god-king was victorious, a triumphal procession, an enthronement, a ceremony to ensure the destinies of the people for the coming year, and a sacred marriage.

Confronted with an alien universe, people—the storytelling animals—described natural phenomena in human terms. Occurrences in nature that frightened and bewildered them were given human shapes and "controlled" through story by means of analogy and metaphor. The clearest forms of such associations are in mythical images where we have "gods" who are human in shape and character, yet identified with something in nature like the sun or the seasons. These myths are metaphors in action, stories about sun gods or fire gods who are human yet totally identified with some force in nature. (Apollo is the sun god and the sun itself.) Simile and metaphor—the primitive and archaic forms of thought used to identify the inner with the outer world—are still used by imaginative writers to suggest an identity between the human mind and the world outside it. In these literary devices, we have another kind of likeness found in literature.

Feeling lost and helpless against the forces of nature, early people told stories of a time when they and nature were in harmony. The story of the Garden of Eden is one such story, but similar ones are found in the mythology of many cultures. The story tells how humans lost their perfect home, became alienated from the rest of the universe and subject to time and death. By the power of imagination, people seek to regain the lost perfect world. In later stories—legends and folktales—the gods take on more human characteristics and have less divine power. Eventually they disappear from stories, and characters become more and more recognizable as limited human beings. Even so, there always exists the desire, expressed implicitly or explicitly in poems, stories, and the lyrics of popular songs, to "get back to the garden." Our literature is a continuous journal of people's search for identity, a metaphorical quest to rediscover a lost perfection, a truly human identity. In modern literature nature is no longer a threat, but the world often seems an alien place, and stories still tell of the individual's efforts to find a place in it. Poet and artist William Blake said, "The nature of my work is visionary and imaginative; it is an attempt to restore what the ancients called the Golden Age."

The Two Rhythms of Literature

For constructing any work of art, we need some principle of repetition or recurrence, like rhythm in music and pattern in painting. In the early development of literature from myth, the storytellers took for their recurring pattern the cycles of nature and eventually made analogies between the natural cycles and the human life cycle.

Mythologies are filled with tales of young gods or heroes—Perseus, Theseus, Jason—who go through various successful adventures, endure great dangers, and are deserted, betrayed, even killed, but who usually emerge safely in the end. The movement of the stories is analogous to the progression of the seasons. The merging of the natural cycle with mythology provided myths with two opposing movements: the rising movement that we find in myths of birth, marriage, and resurrection; and the falling movement in myths of death, metamorphosis, or sacrifice. Later, in stories, they appear as the rising movement of comedy and the falling movement of tragedy.

These early stories reveal another aspect of the human imagination. The hero's quest involves a dialectical or philosophical way of looking at life, reflecting at one limit what people most desire and at the other what they most hate and fear. Myths project a paradise above the world of experience, a place of wish fulfillment in which all obstacles are overcome. Below it, they project a hell, a world of nightmare and bondage. To the quest for identity is added this goal: to reach a state where people are released from an indifferent world into the upper world of their dreams and desires, a world that is the opposite of their nightmares. These two opposing worlds appear in literature as the idealized world of innocence and the absurd, suffering, frustrated world of experience (as illustrated in Figure 4.1).

Out of the cycle of death and renewal and human emotional response to it, there gradually emerged four fundamental patterns of imaginative experience: (1) romance, (2) tragedy, (3) irony-satire, and (4) comedy.

In romance we see how strong and beautiful heroes and heroines set out in search of the ideal green and golden world, the world of forever-summer. Tragedy tells how people, although capable of great things, have limited powers. They are sometimes victims of forces they do not understand and cannot control. Just as the autumn leaves must fall, so they must inevitably move toward death. Irony and satire present the wintry world of experience where life is often as harsh and cruel as the winter winds. In comedy, we find hopeful stories of the renewal of the human spirit. New life springs up as new growth comes again in the spring. Just as the seasons may be considered as distinct though

FIGURE 4.1. Literary Imagery

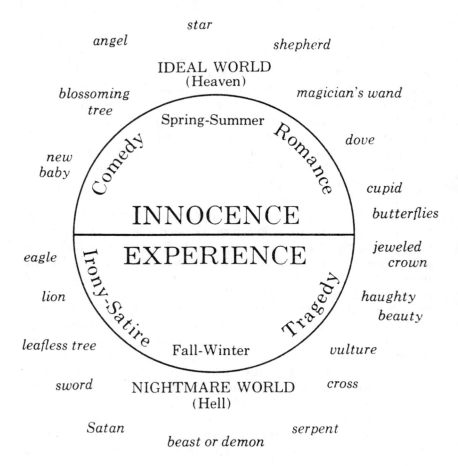

related, so the four imaginative patterns may be seen as aspects of the "one story," people's collective imaginative efforts to give shape to all of human experience. (These four patterns are discussed in detail in Chapter 5.)

John Keats' "The Human Seasons" (1956) is one of many literary works in which the cycles of nature are related to life.

Four seasons fill the measure of the year;
There are four seasons in the mind of man:

> He has his lusty Spring, when fancy clear
>   Takes in all beauty with an easy span:
> He has his Summer, when luxuriously
>   Spring's honied cud of youthful thought he loves
> To ruminate, and by such dreaming high
>   Is nearest unto heaven: quiet coves
> His soul has in its Autumn, when his wings
>   He furleth close; contented so to look
> On mists in idleness—to let fair things
>   Pass by unheeded as a threshold brook.
> He has his Winter too of pale misfeature,
> Or else he would forego his mortal nature.

These two thought constructs (the cycle, together with the image of an upper ideal world and its opposite) underlie all literature. Even a brief lyric poem, although it does not tell a "story," may express the emotions connected with the comic, spring part of the cycle or those related to the wintry world of irony. Because it is so structured, literature is in itself a coherent unity. Within this essentially simple structure one can fit all one's literary experiences. Each poem or story takes on a greater significance when it is seen as part of a whole. The whole is the art of literature, people's imaginative attempt to make sense of the world and their existence in it.

The literature of every culture is shaped by its mythology. Besides being the source of countless allusions in later literature, the Bible and classical mythology supply Western literature with the structure that informs it. The Old and New Testaments of the Bible together provide us with the most complete form we have of the archetypal story of the loss and recovery of identity, the story that is the framework of our literature. The Old Testament begins with the story of the creation of man and woman (Adam and Eve) in paradise, then goes on to tell of their fall from innocence and the loss of their original home. Eventually the story of Adam and Eve becomes the story of Israel, a people who endure a long exile in a wilderness where they cannot feel at home, and who quest to reestablish the ideal world—the rightful kingdom—they once knew here on earth. The New Testament tells of the coming of the second Adam (Christ), who rescues the human race from the wilderness and restores the lost paradise where people are one with themselves and God.

The classical myths give us—more clearly than does the Bible—the main episode of the central myth of the hero whose mysterious birth, triumph, betrayal, death, and rebirth follow the rhythm of the seasons. All stories in literature are developments of fundamental shapes that are seen most clearly in myths, particularly the myth that tells of the quest of the hero.

Displacements from Mythology

Viewed historically, our literature is actually a series of "displacements" from the level of pure myth (religion) to naturalism or realism, the mode of most serious fiction in Western literature for the past 100 years. (Literature for children, until recently comic or romantic, is now increasingly written in the "realistic" ironic-satiric mode.) The images, themes, characters, and plots are "displaced" to make them rationally credible and acceptable to the audience of a particular period, a point that becomes clear when we consider literature both historically and in terms of the principal characters' power in relation to their natural and social worlds.

At the level of pure myth, we have characters who are divine, supernatural figures superior to people and nature. Next come the heroes of epics, who are superior in degree to others and to their environments, moving in a world where the ordinary laws of nature are suspended, and often in close touch with the gods themselves. The next level features princes, kings, and queens, who are portrayed as superior to others but not to their environment. At the next remove, the hero has powers similar to our own. The farthest displacement from myth is a phase of the ironic-satiric mode where we have the anti-hero, who is inferior in power even to ordinary people, a victim of others and the powers of nature.

These levels may be traced through a linear progression in history, one mode dominating in a given period, though not to the exclusion of all other modes. Myth, for instance, prevailed from prehistory to the Middle Ages. Here we have Greek and Roman myths and later those of the Christians. Romance, featuring towering figures like King Arthur and his knights, dominated from the Middle Ages to the Renaissance. The high mimetic mode was dominant from the Renaissance to about 1700, a period that included Shakespeare's great tragic plays about the lives of kings and princes like Lear and Hamlet. Dominant from 1700 to about

1900 was the low mimetic mode, most clearly seen in novels like those of Charles Dickens, which feature ordinary people who cope, mostly satisfactorily, with the problems of ordinary life. Since 1900, the ironic mode, exemplified by the novels of Thomas Hardy, has dominated adult fiction.

In children's literature, which began to appear as separate and distinct from adult literature toward the end of the nineteenth century, the low mimetic mode prevailed until after 1950. Examples of the mode are stories of everyday experiences of ordinary folk by such authors as Louisa May Alcott and Lucy M. Montgomery, followed by Laura Ingalls Wilder, Elizabeth Enright, and Eleanor Estes.

Since 1950, realistic stories for children increasingly have incorporated many of the ironic-satiric elements common to adult fiction. Themes and subjects previously thought unsuitable for children's books are presented with candor—abduction: *The Girl in the Box* (Sebestyen, 1988); rape: *Are You in the House Alone?* (Peck, 1977); racism: *Words by Heart* (Sebestyen, 1979); divorce and abuse: *Holding Me Here* (Conrad, 1986); and the devastation of war: *Hiroshima No Pika* (Maruki, 1980).

Besides ironic realism, contemporary literature for children features historical fiction like *The Sign of the Beaver* (Speare, 1983) and works of fantasy, which include *The Hero and the Crown* (McKinley, 1985) and *Antar and the Eayles* (Mayne, 1990). Both forms permit protagonists the positive heroic action associated with romance and comedy. In stories set in the far past or the faraway future (as in science fantasy), the power of the protagonist is likely to be similar to that of heroes and heroines in the romance and high mimetic modes.

Fantasy may show a dual modality. Child protagonists in the realistic portions of a tale like *The Dark is Rising* (Cooper, 1973) assume the child's role in society, which in general might be characterized as inferior in power to that of adults. However, transported to the fantasy setting of the same story, child protagonists are capable of heroic action. This is true of Max in *Where the Wild Things Are* (Sendak, 1963).

In fantasy that uses diminutive human beings or small animals as characters, the heroic and ironic modes are combined in a single story through manipulation of point of view. Such characters are inferior in power and therefore ironic when seen from the point of view of a human of ordinary size. However, the characters do not perceive themselves as inferior. Since this is so, they may be presented in their story as heroes in the romantic mode. This is true of the child in an early, interesting work of Russell Hoban (1967), *The Mouse and His Child*. Although the child is a windup toy that is cast away in a garbage dump, he has heroic aspirations and is portrayed as having the courage and persistence to achieve them.

Use of diminutive characters and animals provides scope for authors in presenting a child's world. Tiny people and small animals function as metaphors for the child's status in the adult world (Fleming, 1981). But these characters need not be portrayed as victims; through fantasy and manipulation of point of view (the readers' view of the characters and the characters' different view of themselves), they become the take-charge heroes and heroines of romance or the successful survivors of comedy.

Most writers for children, and their publishers, appear unwilling to rob children's literature of its role in educating the young in the positive social and moral ideals of society. In the main, literature for children continues to portray romantic and comic visions of life, where hope and optimism prevail.

CYCLICAL AND DIALECTICAL IMAGERY

As stated in the previous section, the archetypal structures that underlie literary imagery are of two kinds: cyclical (imagery based on natural cycles) and dialectical (images that present contrasting worlds).

Over and over in literature, images of the cycles of nature recur. Countless stories involve a cyclical journey, the hero or heroine returning in the end to the point of departure upon completion of a quest. The pattern of the cyclical journey is common to tales old and new: Odysseus' story shows it, as do *The Tale of Peter Rabbit* (Potter, 1902) and modern fantasies like *Where the Wild Things Are* (Sendak, 1963).

I referred earlier to associations often made in literature between human and animal life and the daily or seasonal cycles. The rejected Ugly Duckling suffers his greatest loneliness in the winter when the ground is frozen and barren. He finds his identity in the springtime in a garden where apple trees are in bloom and the scent of lilac is in the air. When the Norse god Balder lies dead in Asgard, darkness spreads over heaven and earth, the "night of death." Johnny Appleseed dies, but he is memorialized each spring when the apple tree blooms.

In Robert Frost's "Stopping by Woods on a Snowy Evening" (1978), the temptation to give up is associated with winter and the darkest evening of the year. In "Old Man and the Beginning of the World," a myth of the Blackfeet Indians, Old Man promises to return like the sun as he disappears into the west. In more westerns than we can count, the hero rides off into the sunset, not to die but to be reborn in yet another episode of his endless story. The epic hero Gilgamesh, in his quest to find the secret of life and death, follows the "way of the sun" to the Eastern Garden, the sun's dwelling.

Spring and summer are associated frequently with new beginnings, with joy and hope, youth and the prime of life. Autumn and winter are as often associated with old age, death, decay, and loss.

The second major organizing pattern of imagery is revealed through pairs of opposite categories. Above and below the world of human experience, myth projects an upper, desirable ideal world (the heaven of religion) and its opposite, an undesirable nightmare state (hell). The main body of literature is not religious, however, and does not deal with heaven and hell. Instead, the human experience is seen as analogous to these contrasting worlds. William Blake called these human worlds innocence and experience. The imagery of the heavenly world reaches down into the world of innocence; that of the demonic, up into the world of experience (refer to Figure 4.1).

Archetypal Patterns of Imagery

Some important images and their correspondences are presented in Tables 4.1 and 4.2. Table 4.1 shows correspondences between heavenly and demonic images; Table 4.2, between the world of innocence and the world of experience. Table 4.2 relates to Table 4.1, but shows the same images displaced from the heavenly and demonic toward the fantasy world of innocence and the more realistic, human world of experience.

Divine and Demonic Imagery. The heavenly world gives us images of gods like Zeus and the Olympians, a sky-father like Odin, and the three-in-one god of the Christian religion. Its oppo-

TABLE 4.1. Images of Heaven and Hell

	Heavenly	*Demonic*
Divine images	Benevolent gods "above" Luck Angels	Malicious gods "below" Blind fate Devils
Sky images	Sunlight Angels Promethean fire	Darkness Demons and pestilence (as released from ·Pandora's box)
Human images	Humans as community, members of one body The Good Shepherd	Humans as mindless mob The tyrant
Animal images	Lamb, dove	Monsters, birds and beasts of prey
Vegetable images	Garden of Paradise Tree of Life	Wilderness Gallows
Water images	Water of Life	Flood
Mineral images	Temple Jacob's ladder The One Way	Wasteland Tower of Babel The labyrinth

site, the demonic world, features malicious gods like Satan or
mindless forces that are revealed through images of menacing
natural forces, like the sea in the classic, *Call It Courage* (Sperry,
1940). This world may also be represented by a blind, cruel, or
capricious fate against which people and animals have no defenses.
Examples of imagery of the latter type are found in *Faithful
Elephants* (Tsuchiya, 1988), a story based on the killing of the
animals in Tokyo's Ueno Zoo during World War II, and *On My
Honor* (Bauer, 1986), the tragic tale of a child's death and another's guilt.

The innocent world is one of romance or of stories and poems
with a comic or upward movement. The young themselves symbolize innocence. Good parents, wise old men, and benevolent fairy
godmothers are analogous to the divinities of the heavenly world;
false fathers, wicked stepmothers, and ambitious kings, to the
undesirable gods of the demonic world. King Arthur's mentor—
Merlin—and Chiron, instructor of Greek heroes like Achilles and
Jason, are good examples of the wise old men who counsel the

young. The cruel stepmother of "Snow White" and the vicious witch who captures Hansel and Gretel are typical of the heartless hags and other varieties of horrible women whose images haunt the tragic, ironic, sad visions of life.

In *Dorp Dead* (Cunningham, 1965), the evil Kobalt is a literary relative once removed from the wicked sorcerers and wizards of old fairy tales who are themselves one step away from the gods of the underworld. The hunter in the same book who befriends young Gilly provides an opposite image: that of counselor and benefactor. The story takes place in the human sphere but in the character of the hunter is an image that resembles the benevolent deity of the heavenly world.

Sky and Fire Imagery.   Sky and fire images come "down" and "up" from the heavenly and demonic worlds into the literary

TABLE 4.2.   Images of Innocence and Experience

	Innocence	Experience
Divine images	Good parents	False fathers and wicked stepmothers
	Wise old men	Wizards and sorcerers
	Fairy godmothers	Witches and hags
Sky images	Staff, wand	Fiery sword, bombs
	Moon and stars	Jewels and other treasure
	Spirits and fairies	Hobgoblins
Human images	Loving siblings	Wicked stepsisters and stepbrothers
	Wise and helpful men and women	Witches, wizards, temptresses
Animal images	Domesticated animals: dogs, sheep, horses	Birds and beasts of prey
	Unicorns and dolphins	Lions and eagles
Vegetable images	Blossoming tree	Dead tree
	Magician's wand or staff	King's scepter
	Meadows	Gardens and parks
Water images	Warm rain	Sleet
	Water as purifier	Water as destroyer
Mineral images	Paths	Highways
	Country	City
	Mountaintop	Subterranean tunnel

worlds that deal with human concerns. (It becomes clear that knowledge of biblical and classical imagery will make the reading of all subsequent literature more richly meaningful.) In the heavenly sphere we have the sun and the angels, the thunder of Zeus, and Prometheus' gift of the gods' fire to man. There are saints' halos, seraphim and cherubim, ritual sacrifice by fire, and burning bushes.

At the opposite pole is Lucifer and images of consuming fire and brimstone. In between, the world of fire may be represented by malignant demons, will-o'-the-wisps, and burning homes or cities.

In the innocent world fire is usually a purifying symbol, flames that none but the pure may pass through. Sigurd, alone of all the Volsungs, is able to penetrate the wall of fire that surrounds Brynhild. In the story of Sleeping Beauty, the wall of fire is replaced by one of thorns and brambles, but the images are closely related. In the world of experience the heavenly fire blazes in the jewels of the king's crown and the flashing eyes of the beautiful lady.

Human Imagery.   Human images in the heavenly world are those of mankind as members of one body, united in God. At the beginning of the eighth book of the *Iliad*, Zeus remarks that, should he desire to do so, he can pull up the whole chain of being, both gods and humans, into himself, the supreme divine will. There are also images of the Good Shepherd, pastor of a human flock.

In the demonic world the human images indicate disorder and ruthlessness. Among them are cruel tyrants who demand human sacrifices, bloodthirsty mobs, and sirens like those in the *Odyssey* who tempt others to forget their humanity.

In the world of innocence that we see in romance, kings and lords abound, analogous to the gods of heaven. Here the peasant and commoner are idealized, with poor but worthy lads like Boots meeting success against all odds.

In more "realistic" stories in the world of experience there is a closer relationship of imagery to the demonic world. Order and reason and justice do not prevail as in the innocent worlds of comedy and romance. Characters are common and typical men, women, and children subject to all the ills that beset humans. Here characters are more likely to be victims than triumphant heroes. The boy and his family in *Sounder* (Armstrong, 1969), the young escapee from the concentration camp in *North to Freedom* (Holm, 1984), and the abducted child in *Where It Stops Nobody Knows* (Ehrlich, 1988) are examples.

Animal Imagery.   Imagery in the innocent world strongly reflects the biblical and classical. Domesticated animals, notably sheep, are symbols of devotion and loyalty analogous to the Lamb of God. The dove and other gentle birds provide images of peace and love. Unicorns and dolphins contrast with the dragons and monsters of the demonic world. In the Bible we have the monster Leviathan, symbolic of the whole fallen world of sin, tyranny, and death in which man lives. Traditional tales like those of St. George and Beowulf commonly show the heroes fighting evil in the form of dragons and monsters.

Vegetable Imagery.   Vegetable imagery in the heavenly world is well known to us. Both the Bible and classical mythology tell of gardens of paradise. The rose and the lotus are associated with the heavenly world. The tree of life contrasts with the demonic cross. In the human world of innocence, the natural meadow is once removed from the heavenly garden; the more sophisticated cultivated gardens and beautiful parks are associated with the world of experience. In romance, pastoral settings like Sherwood Forest are desirable images. Many modern realistic stories with harsh, bleak urban settings show by contrast that the rural setting is still seen as closer to people's vision of the ideal. A romantic counterpart to the tree of life appears in the wand of the magician and the fairy godmother, which can give life and cause miraculous change.

Demonic imagery is lacking entirely in lush vegetation. Hell is a rocky wasteland where no trees and plants grow or, when they do, their appearance and intent are sinister (the tree of forbidden knowledge, for example). Its counterpart in modern stories of human experience is the concrete and glass city, often depicted as a place of alienation and despair, as in the recent works of Walter Dean Myers, set in the mean streets of the inner city.

Water Imagery.   Water imagery extends all the way from the water of life to the Deluge. In romance literature the hero often descends into or under water, just as the soul of biblical imagery sinks into it at death. For the hero of romance a descent into water may be a kind of ritual death. Mafatu in *Call It Courage* (Sperry,

1940) emerges from submersion in the sea reborn with a new identity.

Water in the world of innocence may be symbolic of growth and fertility or seen, like the biblical ritual of baptism, as a purifier. King Midas must bathe himself in a pool to remove the stigma of the golden touch.

In realistic stories the sea is an adversary to be feared and respected. Water can be shown as the blessing of rain for crops or the destruction of life and property through flooding.

Mineral Imagery.   In the Bible, the mineral world is represented by images of temples and jeweled cities paved with gold. These are reflected in the enchanted towers, castles, courts, and capital cities of romance, and are frequently the goal of young travelers who journey on the highroad in search of treasure or a better life. The highroad itself may be seen as the counterpart of "the one way" of biblical imagery. Demonic mineral images are of deserts, wasteland, swamp, and rocks.

Examples of Archetypal Imagery

Archetypes, the building blocks of literature, are most evident in folktales, fantasy, and formulaic fiction. In the folktale, the romance form—a journey or quest—is typically exemplified. Romance, directly descended from folktale, may be considered the structural core of all fiction: in it we have the fundamental "story" of all literature: the human vision of life as a quest for identity. (See Chapter 5 for a full discussion of the romance structure.) In the quest-romance, the cyclical and particularly the dialectical principles discussed above are evident in all aspects of the tale. The quest is "good," undertaken by one who is worthy. Any person or event that conspires against the success of the quest is "bad." The archetypes recurrent in the tales—and discoverable in the fiction that follows them—reflect this dichotomy. A selection of examples of these patterns follows.

Folktales.   Tales typically feature courageous, innocent protagonists with inherent positive energy or luck, who are often underdogs. Their origins may be humble or mysterious. Pitted against the protagonist are evil villains who block the successful completion of the protagonist's quest. Many tales contain contrasting pairs—usually female—of characters: one good, the other bad.

(Films portraying these "light" and "dark" character pairs, it is interesting to note, frequently cast blondes as the good girls and brunettes as the scheming temptresses.) Often present are wise men or women who watch over or control the action in a positive way, frequently providing a talisman or amulet to aid in the quest. Another archetypal character is one who speaks for the practical and realistic side of things, like Sancho Panza. Common in folktales are helpful animals, spirits, green men, kind daughter figures, creatures of mysterious origin, and the like, who come to the protagonist's aid. In the protagonist's darkest hour, a strange being may materialize, uttering prophecies and oracular sayings.

As for plot, countless folktales (and their descendents in fantasy fiction) feature a series—typically 3, 5, or 7—of combats or tests in which the protagonist is ultimately successful. Parallel plots are common, in which a bad brother or sister may try—without success—to repeat the actions of the good hero or heroine. Common plot devices involve loss and recovery, rescue from evil, twists and reversals of fortune, temptations, and exchanges of various kinds. A final or climactic test of the protagonist often involves a descent into the demonic world, with an eventual ascent that retraces the journey and ends in triumphal completion of the quest. Goodness is rewarded; evil is punished.

Contemporary Novels.   The Mouse and His Child (Hoban, 1967) is a complex example of the romance structure, with that structure's corresponding patterns of imagery and characterization.

The Mouse and his Child, joined together as a windup toy, journey from the harmonious perfection of their early life in the toy shop and the dolls' house down into the demonic world of the garbage dump, which is controlled by satanic Manny Rat, and undergo a further descent into the underworld below the pond before they return to the goal of their quest: to live as a family in the dolls' house with their lost loved ones restored to them.

Despite their misfortunes, the Child is steadfastly optimistic and hopeful for their future. The father Mouse, although supportive, plays the role of realistic advisor when the innocent Child is likely to be disappointed in his hopes.

In the mud below the pond, the Mouse and his Child acquire insight from the oracular wisdom of the turtle, C. Serpentina, and from the Child's own contemplation of infinity in the form of dog food labels on which is printed a picture of a black and white spotted dog in a chef's cap and apron, walking on its hind legs and carrying a tray on which there is another can of Bonzo Dog Food, on the label of which another dog, exactly like the first, may be seen, and so on and on to the last visible dog.

C. Serpentina informs the young mouse that "Nothing is the ultimate truth" (p. 178) but the Child—naively innocent and optimistic like the typical romance hero he is—refuses to accept this. He discovers that he is on the other side of nothing and must help himself; in true heroic fashion, he does. "Nobody can get us out of here but us" (p. 181). Both the Mouse and his Child get out of the mud through the Child's efforts. Images of flying accompany the ascent. The mice fly out of the pond using an invention devised by the Child. Returned to the world of experience, they fly with the hawk to safety.

Helped by gentle animals and birds—a kingfisher, a frog, a bittern—they eventually find their way to the dump and their goal, the dolls' house. Now appropriately painted black, the burnt-out remains of the house are occupied by the monster, Manny Rat. The romantic image of home and haven is replaced by a demonic one of the monster's ugly lair. The protagonists must retrieve the house and restore it. The hero and his helpers battle for the dolls' house, achieving victory—significantly—at dawn.

In the end, the Mouse and his Child, their trials and struggles ended, walk beside the renovated dolls' house, ablaze with electric light, admiring the stars that seem so close to them now that their house is secure on its pole high above the dump. The tramp, the wise old man figure who, at the beginning of the story, mends the Mouse and his Child, appears again at the end, the moment of epiphany, to bless them. The Mouse and his Child have climbed from the depths to the heights to achieve their dream.

The imagery of the dump is demonic imagery of the ironic mode. The divine world, represented throughout by the stars, seems menacing to the evil Manny Rat who "liked dark nights best" (p. 29). Reference frequently is made to Sirius the Dog Star, sacred both to Isis, consort of Osiris, and in Egyptian agricultural rites. References to Sirius suggest that the god is protecting the Mouse and his Child.

The demonic fire world is manifest in the hellish glow arising from the many fires of the dump and from Manny Rat's attempts to blow up the dolls' house. It is also represented positively by the blaze of electricity from the renovated dolls' house. The human world is parodied by the rat society. It is one in which the individual is subordinated to the ruthless power of the leader. Loyalty stems from fear rather than respect. The friends and extended family of the Mouse and his Child present the opposite image of the power of love and mutual aid in overcoming adversity.

The demonic animal world is characterized by monsters and beasts of prey: shrews, weasels, an owl. The ideal animal world features a wise fortune-telling frog, a clever crow who directs the Caws of Art Experimental Theatre Group, a philosophizing muskrat, and a bluejay journalist. The demonic vegetable world is seen in the wasteland and in the symbolic tree of death, here not a gallows but the pole on which the ruined dolls' house perches unsteadily. In their fight to recover the dolls' house from the rats, the animals and birds mount their offensive from an oak tree, which is sacred in folklore as symbol of life and power.

Demonic water images are of death; a flooding dam sweeps the Mouse and his Child into the underworld of the pond. But it is also water that cleanses the dolls' house so the process of restoration can begin.

Only a reading of this intriguing tale can give a full picture of the richness of its contrasting patterns of archetypal imagery, which move from ironic to heroic as the Mouse and his Child are successful in their quest for a home and family.

Dominic (Steig, 1972) shows how another contemporary writer for children makes use of conventional imagery. The hero is Dominic, a cheerful, gregarious mutt who, like countless adventurers, leaves home to seek his fortune: to find adventure and a more satisfying life. Along the way he encounters adversaries, the evil Doomsday Gang: foxes, weasels, ferrets, a wildcat, a wolf, tomcats, dingoes, and rats. The hero and those he befriends in the course of his travels are gentler animals, friendly to people and not given to preying on each other.

Another friend is the archetypal character of the old wise woman, here in the form of an alligator witch. She shares her magic powers with Dominic by giving him her magic wand— wands are fragments of the tree of life—in the shape of a sword that will make him invincible in combat.

Dominic sets out on his adventures along a springtime road strewn with leafy trees and flowers. In this story the forest is sinister, the setting for the hero's greatest trials, confusion, and despair. It is only with great difficulty that Dominic is able to "get out of the woods" to safety. He finds treasure both in the form of diamonds, rubies, and emeralds and in someone to love. His love he discovers in a miniature palace in a beautiful enchanted garden where it is always summer. His dreams of a new and more fulfilling life have come true.

Children's Writings.   An examination of poetry written by children indicates that they have an intuitive grasp of basic patterns of poetic imagery. Just as their first grasp of these patterns in what they read and hear is intuitive, so it is when they write to order their feelings and impressions. The following poems were collected by Robert Wolsch (1970). In the first example loneliness is associated with the cold wind of autumn.

> Child lonely playing
> In the cold and growling wind
> Sees a lone leaf drift.

In another, a child expresses a happy wish of flying high in the sky.

> If I could fly
> I'd roar through the sky
> So high!

The happy freedom of a flying bird contrasts with the sadness of an earthbound boy.

> A beautiful bird
>   flew in the sky
>   and
> A sad little boy
>   sat in the sand. . . .

Natural phenomena are seen as predatory animals.

> The darkening clouds,
> Blot out the sky,
> Thunder roaring like hungry tigers,
> Searching for their prey.
> . . . .

A conscious knowledge of the archetypal patterns of imagery can bring shape and focus to children's writing. Discussion of the symbols and images they will use to express ideas, wishes, dreams, nightmares, and the like will inform their writing and enlighten their appreciation and understanding of the writing of others.

Imagery in Pictorial Art. Archetypal imagery in printed literature must be visualized by the reader or listener. In pictorial art and on film and videotape, however, images are already made visual. The patterns of imagery shown in Figure 4.1 will be found especially in picture books where old folk- and fairytales are retold. The work of Maurice Sendak and Trina Schart Hyman is rich with such images.

In *St. George and the Dragon* (Hodges, 1984, Illustrations by Hyman), the purity and innocence of Una and George, the Red Cross Knight, are reflected in images of flowers, animals like the unicorn and lamb, and the children who welcome them. In his darkest hour, St. George lies wounded under a dark, threatening sky. When he triumphs over the dragon, he is surrounded by images of flowers, of winged beings blowing heavenly trumpets, of sprites and spirits that contrast with the imps and goblins who lurk while he lies wounded.

In *Dear Mili* (Sendak, 1988), a child wanders in a wood of tangled trees and shrubs, birds of prey a threat to her. Yet her guardian angel is near and the threatening wood gives way to images of extraordinary flowers and the light of stars over a cosy cottage where she will find shelter for a time with St. Joseph. When Mili returns at last to her mother's home, the natural images that surround her are autumnal, signalling the death that soon will come to her. In contrast is the bright flower she carries, a gift from St. Joseph that symbolizes the promise of eternal life.

Taken together, the patterns of imagery and the archetypal narrative plots—described in the next chapter—provide a description of the total schematic order found in literature itself. An awareness of the interconnectedness of literary works through recurring and conventional patterns—archetypes—conveys a sense of literature as a unified order of words. This knowledge is crucial to an understanding of the significance of the total body of literature as an imaginative journal of all human experience.

5

The Circle of Stories

> We may feel that this "circle of stories" considerably simplifies the facts of literary experience. Three points in this connection are important. First, the simplification may be valuable for teaching purposes, giving shape and coherence to an inexperienced student's reading. Second, no boundary lines exist, except in diagrams: no classifying or pigeonholing is involved; literary works are simply seen as being in different areas, where they can be both distinguished from and related to one another. Third, and most important, this is not a schematism to be imposed on students. The teacher should have it in mind, but as a principle to give form to his teaching, not as something for the student to memorize and present as a substitute for literary experience.
> —Northrop Frye (1988, p. 118)

The content of each story we read in a book or watch on a screen may be different: The possible combinations of characters and incidents are infinite. What is limited is the number of ways in which stories may be told. Northrop Frye (1957) describes four basic narrative patterns—romance, tragedy, irony-satire, and comedy—that remain constant as the constructive principles used to shape story content; his description is the referent for this chapter.

The four "stories" or plots form a ring or circle of stories (see Figure 5.1). They merge into one another at their limits. Where they overlap we have romantic comedies, for instance, or ironic tragedies.

Within each plot, Frye identifies six separate phases or variations of a central or typical structure—like the quest of romance. However, few works exist in this "pure" form. "The forms of prose

FIGURE 5.1.   The Circle of Stories.

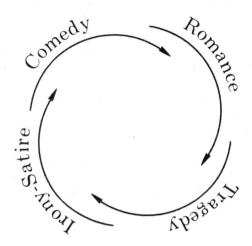

fiction are mixed, like racial strains in human beings, not separable like the sexes" (Frye, 1957, p. 305).

All four plots grow out of the fundamental story of the quest of the hero, as explained in Chapter 4. The circle of stories begins with romance, which develops out of the mythical story of the hero's adventures. His sufferings and trials, his brushes with death, are the focal points of tragedy and irony-satire. The circle ends with comedy, which develops out of the hero's triumph after a successful quest. Taken together, the four basic stories provide an imaginative shape for each aspect of human experience. No one story is the whole. All the stories together are part of the one story: people's quest for their human identity.

ROMANCE

Characteristics

Frye sees romance, considered in formal terms, as the most inclusive literary type. "Romance is the structural core of all fiction: being directly descended from folktale, it brings us closer than any other aspect of literature to the sense of fiction, considered as a whole, as the epic of the creature, man's vision of his own life as a quest" (Frye, 1976a, p. 15). The romance story is one of the great creations devised by the imagination, a form in which wishes come true, goodness always triumphs over evil, and heroes and heroines "live happily ever after" in peace and plenty. Although there are variations within the romance pattern, the central form follows a cyclical pattern involving three principal stages: a dangerous or marvelous journey with attendant preliminary minor adventures (conflict); a central struggle, test, or ordeal (death-struggle); and successful completion of a quest, typically followed by a return to the point from which the journey began (recognition). This complete form is most clearly seen in the stories of the epic heroes: Perseus, Theseus, Jason, Sigurd, Beowulf, Odysseus.

Other stories, actually episodes within the romance form, may tell of the birth of the hero and his early days. His birth, like that of Moses, is often shrouded in mystery and secrecy. Stories of his early life tell of extraordinary powers: Paul Bunyan wields his axe in babyhood; Hercules is still an infant when he strangles the serpents sent by Hera to kill him.

There may be false "fathers" or "mothers" who seek the child's death; Pharaoh, Herod, and the wicked stepmothers of folktales are examples. Often the child is prepared for the illustrious life he will lead by kindly foster parents or wise teachers like Merlin in King Arthur's story.

In variations of the basic romance form, there are stories of innocence pressing toward experience; one contemporary example is *Dicey's Song* (Voight, 1982). In other romance stories, the power of innocence overcomes evil or ugliness, as in *Beauty and the Beast* (Osborne, 1987) or "Soldier Jack" (Chase, 1943).

Since romance is a wish-fulfillment dream, it may also—in some of its forms—show the shadow side of romance: the world we most want to avoid. Here fantasy descends to horror, the principal character doing battle with horrible monsters and giants, perhaps even with death. Romance literature in its demonic vein contains the sinister and horrible images associated with nightmares. Here are tales of the supernatural or of magic powers that operate on the side of evil. Frankenstein is like the scary giants and ogres of fairytales, a dream turned into a nightmare.

On its simplest level the quest is a search for adventure. However, because of its association with the good and the ideal, the quest always has a deeper significance. It is more than adventure for its own sake. Beowulf goes to slay a monster who is laying waste a kingdom; Theseus' goal is to kill the minotaur and put an end to tyranny; Perseus' aim is to destroy the gorgon Medusa whose terrifying visage turns all who look upon her to stone. Countless youngest sons and daughters go forth in folktales to seek their fortunes or a better life. The object of the quest determines the seriousness of the story's tone.

Questers may be rewarded with something tangible: a treasure, a bride, a husband, lands, or a kingdom. They may gain wisdom or magical powers. Whatever the reward, the questing itself is symbolically significant. It represents a journey into the darker regions of experience where the heroes and heroines confront evil and risk annihilation in performing tasks and facing tests that reveal their true relationship to nature, to other people, or to their own selves. Although tangible treasures may result from the quest, perhaps the greatest benefit is the questing character's discovery of self. In its deepest sense, the quest seems to be a search for the knowledge of what it means to be human, of what is involved in taking one's place in the pattern of human civilization as a fully functioning member of society.

The quest may be compared with the rites-of-passage rituals of primitive tribes. Typically the initiates are isolated, given instruction, and made to undergo some ordeal to test strength or wit. When they survive the ordeal, they are reunited with the tribe amid feasting and rejoicing. They may be given new names to symbolize their rebirth as mature members of the society.

The archetype of a questing character is common to all civilizations, from the ancient Babylonians to contemporary primitive tribes. Its ubiquity suggests that the central pattern of romance—the quest—embodies a fundamental pattern of human experience. It has an essential function in the development of the individual's awareness of personal strengths and weaknesses, with psychological as well as ritual or tribal significance.

The two central characters of the romance are heroes or—in many contemporary versions of the form—heroines who are symbolically associated with spring, dawn, youth, and vigor, and their adversaries who are associated with winter, darkness, old age, and sterility. The principal characters of romance are often described as being larger-than-life. They are larger not so much because they are superhuman (though they may possess extraordinary powers) but rather in the sense that they have a vision of a world that is more perfect than the one we live in and a belief in their ability to make that world a reality.

The protagonists of romance are highly idealized figures, usually embodying the virtues held noblest by the societies from which their stories came. They are strong and steadfast, durable and self-controlled. They embody highly civilized virtues like courtesy, wit, and, above all, imagination and vision. Although they may not be gods or even the offspring of gods, they have a mysterious contact with a world beyond the world of experience, from which they seem to derive a power denied to ordinary mortals. Heroic figures radiate a kind of energy, a positive force that bears them forward through all adversity. They are leaders, people at the frontiers of experience. Their triumphs benefit all those around them; their powers lift others toward the heights they scale.

Typical romances move toward progress or fulfillment: victory, the acquisition of treasure, a better life. The achievement involves Herculean efforts on the part of the heroic character, with or without help from others. In the end his or her life is transformed through release from a threatening past or through the realization of some significant understanding.

Most other characters in the romance are one-dimensional. They are either good or bad, for the protagonist or against. Good women in old romances are usually rescued maidens or brides or supporters of the hero; bad women are cast as evil stepmothers, witches, and temptresses. The people who inhabit the pages of romance are not particularly realistic, even in displacements of the form toward "realism." They are more like the desirable characters of our dreams and the undesirable characters of our nightmares.

Romance exhibits a clear up-and-down narrative movement, at times rising into dream or wish fulfillment, and again sinking into anxiety and nightmare. Themes of ascent and descent are common in romance. *Alice's Adventures in Wonderland* (Carroll, 1865/1988) is a case in point; besides Alice's own physical upward and downward movements, there are comings and goings beginning with the fall down the rabbit hole and ending in the eventual ascent into the world of reality. The emphasis on cards and card games relates to the elements of fate and chance in romance.

The settings of early romances—exemplified by folk- and fairytales—are generally idyllic or at least removed from the world of ordinary experience. There are possibilities of magic and miracles. Transformation and metamorphosis are common, as are mistaken identities, disguises, spells, and incantations. Things in nature, trees and animals, often have a mysterious rapport with the heroes or heroines and may provide them with help and advice. Birds warn Snow White of her danger; the Goosegirl has a talking horse as an advocate; Puss in Boots speaks for his master. Traditional tales are full of talking animals who aid the hero. We find this in "The Flea" (Sawyer, 1936), a Spanish folktale, and in the story of Drakestail (Neil, 1986).

Visions and revelations are common to romance. In stories that deal with moral opposites, it is not surprising to find some means of connecting the "heavenly" world with a "lower" one. The union is frequently achieved by a vision or (in more modern romances) an insight that takes place in a high or isolated place like a mountaintop, an island, or a tower. Jacob's ladder is an example of this enjoinment of the two worlds.

Examples of the Romance Form

The Tale of Peter Rabbit (Potter, 1902), durable and delightful, has been a source of literary satisfaction to generations of youngsters. A prime example of the well-constructed story, it exemplifies the romance form in miniature. The hero faces a perilous journey with minor adventures, a crucial struggle, and final exaltation or success, the whole expressing the passage from a point of ritual death to the "resurrection" of the recognition scene.

Peter sets out in defiance of his mother to seek identity, an identity undoubtedly associated with his father who had met an untimely death in Mr. McGregor's garden. The young adventurer undergoes a series of hairsbreadth escapes. He loses his jacket and shoes, is wet and frightened, and escapes only after he finds himself a vantage point that, together with his fleetness of foot, gives him an advantage over his enemy. In the end, as a result of his own efforts, he is safely home, undoubtedly a proven hero, although he has lost his clothes, is not feeling well, and is put to bed with a dose of camomile tea. His well-behaved siblings have bread and milk and blackberries for supper, but it is Peter who is most emphatically the hero of the piece since he is the one who has successfully completed a quest.

The characterization in Peter Rabbit follows the typical conflict pattern of romance. There are two main characters: Peter, the protagonist, and Mr. McGregor, the antagonist. At the lowest point of his trials, when he is imprisoned in the gooseberry net, Peter is encouraged by three friendly sparrows who "implored him to exert himself," characters with literary relatives among the children-of- nature figures common to romance, who are morally neutral and helpful to the hero. The proper siblings are foils for Peter, emphasizing by their docility the enormity of Peter's ambition and daring. The comforting figure of Mrs. Rabbit waiting at home until the hero finishes his wanderings is similar to wife-mother figures in more ambitious and lengthier works: Solveig of Peer Gynt, for example, and Penelope in the *Odyssey*.

For older children, the classic *Call It Courage* (Sperry, 1940) is another example of the romance plot. Mafatu, son of the chief of a Polynesian tribe, lives in fear of the sea, for as a young child he came perilously close to drowning when his mother lost her life as she rescued him. He is reduced to women's work on the island, scorned by his peers as a coward, and a disappointment to his father. The reason for Mafatu's quest is clear—he must find his identity in a face-to-face battle with his enemy, the sea.

Mafatu sets out on his perilous journey, weathering a storm and the destruction of his canoe on a reef. Finally he reaches a desolate island where he sets to work to make a shelter and replacements for the canoe and the weapons he has lost. The sheltering island itself contains a threat, for it is the site of the holy place of sacrifice of a cannibal tribe who will surely return and destroy Mafatu when they know he has desecrated their sacred ground. Yet he sets out calmly to build his boat, gaining courage with every action of his own hand. He kills a wild boar with a weapon of his own making, saves his dog from a tiger shark, and kills an octopus in a daring underwater fight. Drums announce the arrival of the cannibals, but Mafatu's boat is ready and he eludes his pursuers with skill and daring, and sails in the direction of home. He cries out triumphantly to the threatening sea that he no longer fears it, even when there seems little chance of his reaching home again. Mafatu at this moment has won his personal battle and regained his identity. It remains, however, for him to be exalted in the eyes of others, and this happens when he lands safely home, a figure of mystery and magnificence.

In *Call It Courage* the sea is the antagonist, a personification of a being of unlimited strength, bent on destruction. Mafatu's only friends are misfits like himself: a nondescript yellow dog and a lame albatross. Like neutral nature spirits, they play a helping role: comforting the boy, giving him hope and companionship, and—in the case of Kivi the albatross—mysteriously offering guidance as Mafatu begins his quest and ends it.

The romance form is popular in children's literature. It is found in picture storybooks as different as *Where the Wild Things Are* (Sendak, 1963), the delightful melodrama *Brave Irene* (Steig, 1986), and Hardie Gramatky's venerable *Little Toot* (1939). The classical hero tales of Greece and Rome retold in splendid language suited to modern eyes and ears—as in retellings by Ian Serraillier, Roger Lancelyn Green, and Padriac Colum—are superb examples of this form.

Although it may appear with widely different subject matter and express a variety of values, the romance plot pattern has always been a favorite with children and those who write for them. Whether the romance is close to myth and magic like the old tales of heroes, a fantasy, or a realistic modern version of the form, there is no question about its power and importance in the development of the imagination.

Romance tells of dreams and how they are made to come true. It deals in hope. It tells of characters with the courage to prevail when difficulties threaten to engulf them. Romance brings a message from the imagination to the imagination that all children need if they are to slay their personal dragons.

TRAGEDY

Romance, as a story form, tells of wishes and dreams that come true. Poems and stories that explore the limits of people's ability to make their wishes and dreams come true belong to the literary form we call tragedy. Destruction of the innocent, beautiful, or virtuous is something we feel should not happen. Yet such destruction is a fact of the human experience, no matter how wasteful or unjust it may seem. Tragedy, leaving us feeling helpless and vulnerable, reminds us that humans are not omnipotent. Tragic stories sometimes suggest that heroes or heroines are destroyed because they have broken some natural law, even though they may have done so in all innocence. Tragedies are imaginative attempts to balance people's potential greatness with their perishable nature, to come to terms with powers that are greater than theirs.

Characteristics

The central idea of tragedy is catastrophe or death befalling a heroic character. A tragedy may be romantic or ironic and realistic, depending on whether it features idealized or more realistic heroes and heroines. Tragic figures typically endure their trials with the greatest possible dignity; that quality, together with their innocence and courage, claims our empathy for them. Hans Christian Andersen's Steadfast Tin Soldier is such a hero; Balder of Norse mythology is another, as is Barney, the doomed boy in Robert Cormier's contemporary novel, *The Bumblebee Flies Anyway* (1983).

Another form of heroic tragedy is the archetypal story of the loss of innocence, innocence being a lack of experience. Young people can be baffled and hurt by their first contacts with the harsh realities of the world, as is Lena whose life is scarred by racism in *Words by Heart* (Sebestyen, 1979). Such stories may tell of a youthful life cut off or of a child's coming to terms with the untimely death of a loved one.

Still another variation of the tragic story is that of the death, often a willing one, of the hero in support of some great cause. Beowulf deliberately gives his life to save his people. King Arthur knows that his whole life has been a sacrifice for a "dream of justice." This type of tragic story derives from the ancient ritual of the scapegoat: The evils of the tribe were ritualistically invested in an animal who was then driven into the wilderness to die. In the tragedy of sacrifice, the hero's society is purged of evil by his sacrifice, voluntarily made on behalf of his people.

The tragedy of sacrifice is a grave reminder of what it costs to be fully human in the noblest sense. The heroic characters accept fate and resist oppression, willing to risk or lose their lives for a great cause. Theirs is a sobering story but an exhilarating one, found in both epic tales like *Beowulf* and biographies of such men and women as Martin Luther King, Jr., Malcolm X, and the celebrated savior of slaves, Harriet Tubman.

Many tragic stories center around characters who are not of the world of innocence but of the world of experience. They are puzzling characters; they may be great leaders and in many respects heroic, but at the same time their character or outlook contains a flaw that leads them to make some disastrous mistake or choice. Their action appears to provoke a situation that causes their inevitable downfall, a sense of their having disturbed the natural order. Such stories seem to tell of a kind of revenge, a hostile reaction from some power that is beyond them. Great classical tragedies like *Antigone* and *King Lear* belong in this category.

As tragedy gets closer to irony in the circle of stories, heroes become more lifelike, no longer the larger-than-life figures just spoken of. Here are stories that reflect people's sense of being caught in a trap from which they cannot free themselves, of being victims of vast and overwhelming forces that immobilize and imprison. In ironic literature, we see the human spirit defeated under similar conditions. But in tragedy, even when all hope is lost, people retain their human dignity. By the very act of facing the realities and challenges of life, the characters triumph over them.

Elements of Tragedy in Children's Literature

William Armstrong's *Sounder* (1969) illustrates this last type of tragic story. The father, a black sharecropper in Louisiana during the Depression, is a victim of circumstances beyond his control. His opportunities are limited. Both nature and men are hostile. The land bears poor crops, and no one comes forward to help him feed his starving children; when he steals food for them, his captors are ruthless in their punishment. Yet he endures through agonies of pain when the posse's guns injure him and through the knowledge of his family's suffering when he is taken off to prison. He returns home, body broken but spirit intact, to die with dignity, leaving that and his courage as a legacy of hope to his children.

The full power of the tragic form is seldom experienced in children's literature, except perhaps in myths, legends, and epics. However, many modern children's stories contain elements of tragedy, notable among them Ouida Sebestyen's *Words by Heart* (1979). Set in cotton country at the turn of the century, it tells the story of Lena, a young black girl whose special talent is reciting scripture. Eager to earn her father's admiration and to make her white classmates notice her "Magic Mind," not her black skin, Lena sets out to win a Bible-quoting contest.

Lena wins, but winning does not bring her the expected acceptance and praise. Instead, her triumph forces her to acknowledge bitter truths: The people of the town begrudge her winning; worse, they resent her family's presence in the all-white town where her idealistic, pacifist father has settled them. Her father's ideals and good intentions cannot hold up against prejudice and bigotry. In the end Lena is left to reconcile herself to grief and bitterness at her father's murder.

Tragedy, in contrast with irony, does not leave us with a sense of hopelessness. The tragic figure may suffer, even die, but he or she characteristically displays the highest of human attributes: nobility and dignity. In *The Bumblebee Flies Anyway* (Cormier, 1983), 16-year-old Barney, finally accepting—after a period of desperate denial—the bleak truth that his own death is imminent, forgets himself in his heroic efforts to bring happiness to a friend in the last moments of both their lives.

SATIRE AND IRONY

Satire and irony are literary forms set in the world of experience, reflecting the discrepancy between what is and what ideally ought to be. Satire attempts to change people and society for the better, often by using ridicule to expose follies and hypocrisies. Satire may employ fantasy; irony deals in realism.

Both forms typically parody the themes and patterns of romance to make their points. Protagonists are not larger-than-life; they are all-too-human, subject to all the ills of the world: physical weakness, other people's inhumanity, their own neuroses. Time passes and they must grow old and die. There is no feeling, as there is in tragedy and romance, of mysterious powers that link these people to something that transcends the world. Since they are merely human in a world that is far from ideal, their quests frequently remain unfulfilled as they pursue unrealistic goals or proceed wrong-headed and misdirected.

The heroic qualities of the main characters of romance are absent in the anti-heroes of irony or are employed by the hero-as-rogue who outwits the unscrupulous by becoming unscrupulous himself. The good and innocent are more likely to be victims than champions, and love is more often thwarted than conquering. The green world of romance is replaced by the harsh concrete of the city slum.

Satire

The satirist chips away at the huge ills of humanity: hypocrisy, self-deceit, smugness, pettiness, injustice. In some satires, people are shown accepting what they believe cannot be changed or retreating into rationalizations in an effort to escape. There are stories granting that the world is full of crime and folly, but counseling readers to laugh at the follies around them. Through humor and exaggeration, the satirist's audience has its consciousness raised and its perceptions sharpened.

Most satire is beyond the imaginative reach of young children, and few authors write in this form for them. The satiric aspects of *Gulliver's Travels* (Swift, 1726/1985) and *Alice's Adventures in Wonderland* (Carroll, 1865/1988) are for the most part absorbed without notice as the stories are enjoyed for their own sake. "The Emperor's New Clothes" (Andersen, 1974) is a notable exception, where children encounter satire in a form more manageable by them. Elements of satire occur, however, in contemporary children's fiction like *The Wish Giver* (Brittain, 1984), *The Whipping Boy (S.* Fleischman, 1987), *The Shrinking of Treehorn* (Heide, 1971), *Konrad* (Nostlinger, 1977), and *The Pushcart War* (Merrill, 1964).

Satire, in literature for children, is usually softened through fantasy and humor. Both *Konrad* and *The Pushcart War* are excellent examples. *Konrad* is a thoroughly delightful spoof on the wonders of a technological society that can produce anything, even children made to order in factories. The highly original classic, *The Pushcart War,* features a brave army of pushcart owners who outwit big business in New York City.

Irony

Ironic stories, like satiric ones, take place in the world of experience rather than in the world of innocence, and with them too, heroism is impossible. They differ from satire in that no moral ideal seems possible.

Since the 1960s, much children's literature has been written in the ironic mode of most contemporary adult literature. *The Pigman* (Zindel, 1968), a story written for young adolescents, looks at tragedy from below, from the moral and realistic perspective of the state of experience. It stresses the humanity of its heroes, minimizes the sense of ritual inevitability found in tragedy, and supplies social and psychological explanations for catastrophe.

In *The Pigman*, two precocious, perceptive, lonely teenagers make friends with an equally lonely, strange old man, Mr. Pignati, who lives only through dreams of his dead wife and daily visits to his closest friend, a baboon at the zoo. The story is narrated alternately by the hero and heroine in a series of flashbacks, their attempt to make sense of all the crazy things they did. It is often funny in its digressions, wit, and candor, but the humor only serves to point up the irony that underlies it.

Alienated from their parents, John and Lorraine find in the Pigman someone who accepts them as they are, spoils them a little, and genuinely enjoys their company, luxuries not to be found in their homes. Their zany relationship flourishes in love and laughter; they have the run of his cluttered old house, sharing with him food and trips to the zoo. He buys them gifts of roller skates, and all three joyously skate down the hallway of his home. Human weakness and poor judgment are their undoing. Mr. Pignati suffers a heart attack after a hilarious skating session. While he is hospitalized, John and Lorraine invite friends to a party that turns his house into a shambles. His wife's collection of prized china pigs is smashed, her clothes ripped by the girls who dress up in them, and his belongings looted. In the midst of the chaos Mr. Pignati returns from the hospital. Although he forgives the stricken young people, who are not sure how things got so far out of their control, his gay spirit is broken. When they persuade him the next day to take a trip to the zoo to see Bobo, his baboon friend, he agrees half-heartedly to go. Once there he discovers that Bobo died while he was in the hospital. Mr. Pignati, weak from the heart attack, dies in front of the baboon cage.

John tries to sum up his feelings at the end, deploring life "in a world where you can grow old and be alone and have to get down on your hands and knees and beg for friends" (p. 144). He muses that, for that matter, maybe he and Lorraine are baboons, only of a different kind, and that his parents and everyone else are "baffled baboons concentrating on all the wrong things" (p. 145). The young people have faced reality and themselves, and found both confrontations unpleasant.

It is interesting to note that in a sequel to *The Pigman*, *The Pigman's Legacy* (Zindel, 1980), the unrelieved irony of the first book is tempered with humor. However, problematic aspects of living—as diverse as health care, communication gaps between the generations, and paying taxes—are examined through satire. In the circle of stories, the second story—though still in the ironic-satiric mode—is closer to comedy, ending as it does with hope and a promise of love, which John and Lorraine have come to realize is the Pigman's legacy.

Simple though it is, the familiar tale of The Gingerbread Boy is a good primer introduction to the ironic form. The Gingerbread Boy, about to be eaten, escapes and rolls down the hill on a quest for freedom and safety, narrowly escaping all who would eat him, and that is everyone he meets, including the family from whom he first escaped. Freedom seems certain until the Gingerbread Boy makes a friend of Piggy Wiggy—in some versions, Fox—who proves false. In the process of what seems a helpful act of carrying the Gingerbread Boy on his snout in order to cross a brook, the pig swallows him in one gulp. The Gingerbread Boy's quest is cut short unfulfilled.

Other stories in the ironic mode include Marilyn Sachs's *The Bears' House* (1971), Louise Fitzhugh's *Nobody's Family Is Going to Change* (1974), and *Mrs. Fish, Ape, and Me, the Dump Queen* (Mazer, 1982). The novels by Fitzhugh and Mazer illustrate how humor is often used to ease the pain of "telling it like it is" in stories for young people.

The ironic mode is further accommodated in children's stories that use toys, animals, and diminutive people as protagonists. In this mode the protagonist is inferior in power even to ordinary people, a victim of others and the powers of nature and inferior in power and intelligence to the reader, who has the sense of looking down on a scene of entrapment, frustration, and absurdity.

However, the animals, toys, or diminutive characters do not necessarily see themselves as ironic victims (Fleming, 1981). Rather, like William Steig's *Dominic* (1972), they may perceive themselves as protagonists in the adventurous world of romance, in which danger is great but honorable motives, courage, and determination are rewarded. Excellent examples of such protagonists are found in *The Borrowers* (1953) and its several sequels, written by Mary Norton, and in *The Mouse and His Child* (Hoban, 1967).

By using animals, toys, or diminutive characters as protagonists, authors are able to present, through the fantasy, an ironic view of life, while at the same time preserving the optimism and positive values of the comic and romantic modes, traditionally considered the most appropriate for children's literature. "If inferior in power or intelligence to ourselves, so that we have a sense of looking down on a scene of bondage, frustration, or absurdity, the hero belongs to the ironic mode" (Frye, 1957, p. 34). In the reader's eyes, the Mouse and his Child have ironic status because they are powerless, unable to move unless someone winds them up. However, they—like other toy and animal characters or diminutive people in stories—do not have an ironic view of themselves. Their positive viewpoint enables them to behave like heroes and heroines. Indeed, the Child undertakes a heroic quest and is successful in it.

Ironic stories typically reveal a bitter picture of existence: the contrast between ideals and reality. Some believe that children's literature must reflect life "as it is" and not see it through the rose-colored glasses of romance and comedy. There is merit in this view, of course, but irony and satire do not present the whole story of the human experience any more than romance and comedy do. Irony, in fact, proves to be romance turned upside down, the nightmare instead of the dream. Implicit in the ironic story is the dream of how things "ought to be."

COMEDY

When we speak of comedy, we are likely to think of laughter, but many forms of the comic plot in literature are not necessarily comical or humorous. They do, however, present a positive view of the human experience. Comedy is a form that celebrates the power of nature, human or otherwise, to renew itself, the power of life to overthrow the threat of death. It has to do with transformation, with the power of the imagination to raise experience above the limits of time and space, and to change the undesirable into the desirable.

Characteristics

The central idea of comedy is rebirth or renewal after obstacles have been overcome. The simplest pattern of comedy is expressed in the old cliche: boy meets girl, boy loses girl, boy and girl are reunited. Protagonists are kept from the object of their desires by a series of blocks or obstacles, often in the form of intransigent antagonists. The comic form usually involves a movement from one kind of society to another: from the rule of impossible, unreasonable people to the establishment of a new order where everyone is happy.

This ending is achieved by almost any means: miraculous transformations, coincidences, magical interventions. But the audience is delighted even when the solution is improbable, because they know that this is the only possible ending, the way things "ought to be." Even the intransigent characters are reformed and redeemed and become part of the new social order in the end, like Scrooge in *A Christmas Carol* (Dickens, 1843/1952).

The typical hero of comedy resembles Wilbur in E. B. White's *Charlotte's Web* (1952): well-meaning, likeable enough, but rather ordinary. Wilbur is aided by a cunning cohort, Charlotte, a character type common to comedy and related to the "tricky slave" of ancient Roman comedies, whose wit and daring frequently saved his charming but none-too-bright master. The chief blocking character is often a father figure or an outright villain, or is represented by an unfair or impossible situation that must be overcome, like the threat to Wilbur's life. Other comic characters include detractors of the hero, like Templeton the rat, and buffoons who contribute to the comic action with singing, clowning, and miscellaneous humor, like the gossipy goose in *Charlotte's Web*.

Like tragedies, comic plots may stretch from the limits of the ironic to the romantic. Julia Cunningham's *Dorp Dead* (1965) is an ironic comedy where the will to live triumphs over odds that must surely have left scars. Books like *Charlotte's Web, The Trumpet of the Swan* (White, 1970), and *Sarah, Plain and Tall* (MacLachlan, 1986) are romantic comedies at the other end of the scale; from beginning to end their mood is one of hope.

Examples of the Comic Form

An excellent example of the comic structure in children's literature is one of the first books by Dr. Seuss, *The 500 Hats of Bartholomew Cubbins* (1938), a venerable favorite that is a comedy in the phase closest to romance. In this story there is a magical element that is never explained: the 500 hats that appear successively on Bartholomew's head are a phenomenon that "just 'happened to happen' and was not very likely to happen again" (unpaged).

Bartholomew, much like the heroes of Dickensian comedy, is a likeable chap, unpretentious and brave enough when he must be. Through no fault of his own, he is confronted with a wrathful and unreasonable king who demands that Bartholomew remove his hat in the king's presence. The hero tries to comply but cannot; whenever he removes his hat, another appears in its place. Like the hero of a picaresque tale, a juvenile Tom Jones, he is whirled off into a series of adventures, more or less an innocent victim of circumstances and situations largely beyond his control.

The characters are typical figures of comedy. The king is a blustering and unreasonable figure, foolish in his repeated attempts to divest Bartholomew of his offending hats. His retinue includes buffoon types reminiscent of the cooks and clowns of Shakespeare: the pompous prime minister, the ineffective and comical wise men and magicians.

Bartholomew faces death bravely and calmly enough in his stolid way, until he is saved—in the nick of time—by the magical powers that brought him into danger in the first place. The final hats grow more and more magnificent until the vain and greedy king, behaving true to character, covets one for his own. He pays Bartholomew a substantial sum for the splendid five hundredth, places it over his crown, and is appeased at last. Arm in arm, he and Bartholomew gaze out over the royal domain from the same vantage point, as equals. How such a reversal is accomplished is inherent in the comic structure itself. Everything moves toward the "happy ending," with the blocking characters converted at last to the hero's side.

The old tale of Cinderella is a prime example of the comic structure, its pattern enduring in displacements old and new and yet to come. It exemplifies comedy in the phase closest to romance, for it involves magical manifestations and metamorphoses. The worthy Cinderella endures against impossible odds, powerless against the cruel and unreasonable treatment of her stepmother and stepsisters who thwart her every wish and desire, including preventing her attendance at the prince's ball. Then her goodness is rewarded; her fairy godmother transforms her utterly. She must do as she is told (and she is used to that) and all will be well.

Cinderella at last is received into the society in which we all knew from the beginning she belonged; it is in effect a movement from illusion to reality. The illusion is always negative forces that must be dispelled, caused as they are by hypocrisy, injustice, and the like. Cinderella, of course, was really a princess in disguise. In the end, the prince recognizes this, and the king and queen receive her as if she were a long-lost daughter; even her stepmother and wicked stepsisters share in her triumph in most versions. The character of Cinderella is the embodiment of the wish fulfillment: Virtue and goodness are rewarded; things turn out "as they should."

The comic form is a favorite of writers for children, found in countless traditional tales like *Beauty and the Beast* (Osborne, 1987) and *Snow White and the Seven Dwarfs* (Grimm, 1886/1972) and in tales of survival—a popular theme for children's fiction—

like Gary Paulsen's *Hatchet* (1988) and Elizabeth Speare's *Sign of the Beaver* (1983).

The main emphasis in comic literature, then, is on the creation of a new or better order or set of circumstances. This is often achieved by equating the new and better world with the season of spring, a time of beginnings and renewal. The world at the end of a typical comedy is renewed, better and more ordered, freer and more merciful than the old order it replaces. The marriage and the happy ending typical of comedies are symbolic of the establishment of a new, more just society.

The biblical Book of Revelation uses the marriage metaphor to symbolize an eventual happy ending to the human story. A bride from earth, known variously as the new Jerusalem, the church, or the community of saints, is united with the redeemer and with him enters paradise. The central form of the comic story is symbolic of hope, of possibilities for new and renewed life, of triumph over trials and difficulties, and of the power of love.

SUMMARY OF THE FOUR PLOTS

The main idea of romance, the first story, is adventure or action. An innocent, idealized person moves in a world beyond the ordinary and realistic world of experience and undergoes a quest involving a test of his or her human powers. The central idea of tragedy, the second story, is catastrophe or death befalling a hero who maintains those qualities humans consider heroic no matter what the hero's fate. Tragedies may be romantic or ironic depending on whether they feature idealized characters or more realistic ones. The controlling idea of satire and irony is the absence of heroism and the presence of chaos, confusion, misery, and injustice—the world of experience. Satire attempts to change the unsatisfactory condition by revealing through ridicule such things as hypocrisy. Ironists simply show things as they see them, and their point of view is a negative one. Comedy, the fourth story, moves out of ironic confusion; its central idea is the human spirit's potential for renewal. It ends with a transformation of ironic chaos. The comic spirit is one of hope for the future and faith in human endurance over time.

The stories that people tell are parts of a single story. That one story is people's search for human identity, a search that continues

and will continue as long as there are people. It begins with an ideal
world, moves through the less perfect world of human experience,
and toward a vision of the return of the perfect harmony of Eden.
There are moments when we catch a glimpse of that perfect world.
For it exists in the minds of imaginative writers and in imaginations awakened by their words.

IMPLICATIONS FOR TEACHING AND LEARNING

Figure 5.2 is at once a review of the characteristics of the plot
of each of the four narrative types and an example of an exercise
in criticism undertaken by middle school students. These questions were developed by Cathy Swan's sixth-grade reading
class in New Canaan, Connecticut, to be used as the basis for
small-group discussion of stories and novels. John Willinsky (in
press), after observing a class at work putting a story to the "test,"
noted that the exercise brought the class to the brink of literary
knowing, in this case to a sense of symbolic meaning.

> A number of the students also took that extra step beyond nam-
> ing the right archetype for the story. They were practising lit-
> erary criticism, with their insights slipping out off-handedly. . . .
> Such is the elusive nature of teaching and learning. But there
> is the added point here that within this theory of literature is
> buried the idea that these insights aren't directly about anything
> so much as the pattern of literature.

The unifying principles of literature provide an organiza-
tional scheme that enables students to see literature as a whole
rather than as a collection of unrelated entities. It provides a way
of relating together all the verbal constructs of our experience—
both literary and subliterary—thereby providing a sense of the
scope and extent of the human imagination as it works in creating verbal structures.

Identification of patterns and relationships is one of the major
ways in which we learn. In discovering the patterns and interrelationships of literary works, students have a more-than-usual sense
of the importance of literature as a study. For the whole—like a
jigsaw puzzle—makes sense only when the right context is found
for each of its parts.

An understanding of the unifying principles of literature lib-
erates criticism because it provides a view that comes from step-

FIGURE 5.2. Determining Characteristics of the Four Narrative Types

Romance Test

1. Was there a quest?
2. Does the main character have supernatural powers or special abilities?
3. Is the setting a fantasy (a dream or nightmare) world?
4. Does good triumph over evil?
5. Does the main character "live happily ever after"?
6. Do wishes come true?
7. Did the story make you feel that you can slay dragons?

Tragedy Test

1. Does the story show the main character's limits?
2. Does the main character have a fault?
3. Does the main character make a disastrous choice or mistake?
4. Does the choice or mistake affect the natural order?
5. Does the main character seem to be caught in a trap?
6. Does the main character die in the end?
7. Does the main character exhibit dignity and honor?
8. Does the story remind you that people have limitations?

Irony-Satire Test

1. Is the story set in the world of experience?
2. Does it discuss human limitations?
3. Is the main character all-too-human?
4. Is the main character a hero or a champion?
5. Does the quest remain unfulfilled?
6. Is the setting cold?
7. What is being attacked satirically?
8. Does the story attempt to change people's behavior?
9. Is there hope in the end?
10. Did the story teach you that we must fight the ills of humanity? How?

Comedy Test

1. Does the story show a positive view of life?
2. Is the main character likeable but ordinary?
3. Is there a clever, daring side-kick who saves the main character?
4. Does the story have a blocking character or situation?
5. Are there detractors who keep the main character from his/her goal?
6. Is there a major transformation?
7. Does this transformation seem magical or miraculous?
8. Do blocking characters convert to the main character's side?
9. Is there a happy ending with a move toward a better life?
10. Does the story teach you that with love and hope you can make a better life?

ping back from the works to better see their organizing structure and how they fit with respect to other works. It is not meant as a system to justify pigeonholing—paring and prodding each poem, play, and story until it fits into a slot. It releases students from the stultifying, myopic study of literature that centers in recall of bits and pieces of a work's content. It provides a way to broaden the perspective of discussions about literature.

These principles are not to be learned by rote. What they can do is provide the teacher with a deductive framework to keep in mind during discussions with students. For the students, learning proceeds inductively; from broad experience with literature and nonliterary forms of daily experience, they begin—with guidance—to see for themselves patterns and relationships in what they read, see, and hear and to make generalizations. Students know a great deal more than they realize; their verbal experience has been built up by reading, listening to stories and conversation, watching movies and television, and listening to the lyrics of pop songs. The teacher—informed by a knowledge of literature's unifying principles—helps students to discover and express their knowledge. With the realization that literature is a coherent order of words comes a greater sense of its significance as a study and of its importance in our lives.

This realization grows out of experience. Experiencing imaginative literature is therefore the first step in the development of the child as critic. The focus in this book is on imaginative literature for several reasons.

The first reason is obvious: poetry and story appeal to children. Furthermore, the best poems and stories are illustrative of the wonders and marvels that may be created with words. Since they are born of the imagination, they have the potential for educating that faculty in readers and listeners. In addition, the unifying principles of literature are revealed through experience with poetry and story. Accordingly, the next two chapters (in Part III) are about the first aspect of criticism, experiencing literature. In Chapter 6, poetry is considered; Chapter 7 focuses on story.

PART III

Theory Into Practice

6

Poetry and Literacy

Poetry, the main body of which is verse, is always the central powerhouse of a literary education. It contributes, first, the sense of rhythmical energy. . . . It contributes too, as the obverse of this, the sense of leisure, of expert timing of the swing and fall of cadences. Then there is the sense of wit and heightened intelligence, resulting from seeing disciplined words marching along in metrical patterns and in their inevitable right order. And there is the sense of concreteness that we can get only from the poet's use of metaphor and visualized imagery. Literary education of this kind . . . can do something to develop a speaking and prose style that comes out of the depths of personality and is a genuine expression of it.

—Northrop Frye (1963b, p. 26)

In most classrooms, poetry, far from being a central power-house in literacy education, seldom plays even a small part in efforts to promote reading and writing ability. Few studies have been undertaken on its motivational potential for encouraging reading and writing or on its role in developing facility in language, probably because poetry generally is not considered a major factor in elementary programs to develop literacy. Of all the forms of literature, poetry is farthest removed from the practical and prosaic and therefore easily shunted aside in a short-sighted curriculum that sees it as a decorative distraction from the pursuit of utilitarian "language arts" and "communication skills."

THE PRIMACY OF POETRY

Formal literacy education typically begins with the inauthentic prose of the basal reader. In misguided efforts to teach the basics from a utilitarian base, we overlook what is truly basic—the child's natural propensity for the poetic: metaphoric expression, rhythm, rhyme, pun, riddling, wordplay in all its forms (Geller, 1985).

Generally, our notions about language are prose-based. Early in our education we become familiar with the distinction between poetry and prose. Along with the recognition of this distinction usually comes the conviction that prose is the language of everyday speech and is therefore the more natural means of expression. Poetry, as misguided in-school attempts to uncover and explain its "true" or "hidden" meaning seem to indicate, is widely considered to be an almost perverse—albeit often witty and ingenious—way of distorting prose statements. However, the truth is that prose, like poetry, is far from being the language of everyday speech.

> Prose is not ordinary speech, but ordinary speech on its best behavior, in its Sunday clothes, aware of an audience and with its relation to that audience prepared beforehand. It is the habitual language only of articulate people who have mastered its difficult idiom. (Frye, 1963b, p. 18)

Ordinary speech is characterized by short phrases, sketchy syntax, and repetitiveness, with many of the repetitions, like nonsense words in verse, serving as rhythmical filler. This teenager's speech is an example: "Like, I mean, the new guy is cute. Know what I mean?"

Verse and prose are both used to regulate and control the babble of speech. Prose, however, is the more difficult way to conventionalize it. Historically, verse precedes prose in a society's literature, often by centuries. Primitive poetry delights in catalogues: long lists of strange names, names that are potent in magic, that are keys to history, that summon up the deeds of heroes and gods. In this poetry everyday language is conventionalized, ordered to form, shaped, and controlled. Children, on their own, recapitulate the experience of primitive literature, turning easily toward the conventionalized, to riddles, chants, conundrums, and jingles (Opie, 1959). If their natural speech is any indication, young children understand that verse is a more direct way of conventionalizing speech than is prose.

Poetic Devices in Children's Speech

In poetry and in children's talk, abstractions are visualized and personalized; logic and sequence are subordinated to the insights of metaphor and simile. Figures of speech are seen for what they are, direct means of expression, rather than ornaments of language.

The poet, like the child, works with sensory experience rather than abstractions, using images rather than ideas and concepts. The poet typically employs the most primitive of categories, similarity and identity. Something is like something else or something is something else. "Like a small grey/coffee-pot,/sits the squirrel," says Humbert Wolfe (1962, p. 303); Vachel Lindsay tells us that 'The Moon's the North Wind's cooky" (1983, p. 30). A child with a stomachache complains that his stomach is "broken." Another, looking in awe at her grandmother's varicose veins, asks why her legs are all "thunder and lightning."

That children love riddles is one indication of their poetic turn of mind. The riddle's use of pun and identification reflects the mental processes of young children. In a riddle what is being described is not the thing itself but its properties and effects, as in this riddle about a well: "As round as an apple, as deep as a cup, / And all the king's horses can't pull it up." Children's naturally metaphoric way of looking at things makes the riddle an appealing form for them. The riddle, where something is described in terms of something else, embodies the very essence of poetic thought.

If younger children's metaphoric sense is capitalized upon and preserved through riddles and other poetic forms, instead of finding the advanced study of poetry difficult, as those raised on textbook prose often do, they will recognize its associations and identities as the simple, natural, and direct forms of expression with which they are familiar.

Other poetic devices—rhythm, alliteration, onomatopoeia— are also natural elements of the child's own expression, which is repetitive, heavily accented, given to sing-song, whine, and croon. The following examples are from studies by graduate students in my classes at Queens College:

- Several students described how young children take a phrase or word, heard but not necessarily understood, and make a chant of it. One 2-year-old stamped around the backyard to "Zilch, zilch, zilch-zilch-zilch."
- An example of wordplay comes from a 7-year-old helping to carve a pumpkin: "The stuff inside is like orange gunk; it's like orange gook; it's like orange gluk; it's like orange glunk."
- Onomatopoeia is in a 5-year-old's account of how Tommy fell in a puddle: "Yeah! Tommy was riding SWISH! down past Roz and hit a rock SMASH! (smacks hands together) The bike fell over into that big muddy puddle—KSHHH!"
- There is rhyme in a 4-year-old's conversation with a bug: "Hello, bug wug. Buggy, wuggy, bug, wug. Glug!"
- Examples of rhythm, rhyme, alliteration, and assonance abound in playtime chants and jingles such as

  > Baby, baby, stick your head in gravy;
  > Wrap it up in bubble gum,
  > And send it to the navy.

As these examples from their speech and oral lore indicate, children are explorers of language. They love to pun, to play with words, to ask riddles featuring words that sound the same but have different meanings: "Why did the house call the doctor?" "Because it had a window pane." Like poets, children are fascinated by all the marvelous things that words can do: how sounds mimic what is being described, how puns are possible, how language can be made to "natter, patter, chatter and prate" (Merriam, 1974, p. 4).

In simpler societies poetry emerges as a primary need because it is seen as a simple and direct means of expression. In Eskimo, for instance, the word *anerca* means "poetry"; it also means "to breathe." Children seem intuitively to understand that metaphor, far from being mere decorative language, is a powerful means of linking thoughts to experience. One child, during a ride in a car, commented that the "road is a big waist and we're riding on the belt."

Primitive poetry is linked to movement, to the basic bodily rhythms involved in singing, dancing, marching. Children are kinesthetic creatures who delight in moving to rhythmic chants of words that take their fancy. Polysyllabic mouthfuls become rhythmic background for table-beating and pan-pounding. Children know how language and movement relate. They bounce balls and

skip rope in time to chanted words; they tease in taunting rhythmic rhymes. They call on the magical powers of incantation.

> White horse, white horse,
> Bring me good luck;
>> Good luck to you,
>> Good luck to me,
>> Good luck to everyone I see.

In young children, movement and language are inextricably
bound.

Implications for the Classroom

> Ideally, our literary education should begin not with prose, but
> with such things as "This little pig went to market"—with verse
> rhythms reinforced by physical assault. The infant who gets
> bounced on somebody's knee to the rhythm of "Ride a cock
> horse" does not need a footnote telling him that Banbury Cross
> is twenty miles northeast of Oxford. . . . All he needs is to get
> bounced. If he is, he is beginning to develop a response to
> poetry in the place where it ought to start. For verse is closely
> related to dance and song; it is also closely related to the child's
> own speech. (Frye, 1963b, p. 25)

Poet Eve Merriam also emphasizes the importance of experiencing poetry physically: "There's a physical element in reading poetry aloud; it's like jumping rope or throwing a ball" (Sloan,
1981, p. 959). She advises young poets not to intellectualize, but
to respond to words with movement: "Use your whole body as
you write. It might even help sometimes to stand up and move
with your words" (p. 963).

To fail to capitalize on children's poetic language sense is a
serious mistake. Good writing is based on good speech; the good
speech of each individual is a direct reflection of personality. If
we write in a way we never speak, our writing is sure to lack
conviction and individuality. Rhythmic poetry can give children
a sense of their own inner rhythms. Far from being frills on the
edge of a literacy program, these activities—hearing verse, repeat-
ing it, moving to it, letting the music of the language sink in until
it becomes part of you—are the power sources that fuel it.

It is an educational truism that we must begin instruction
when children are in their development. Imaginative literature is

exactly where they are. It makes good sense to have children read and listen to poetry, because verse is closer to their natural mode of expression than more utilitarian forms of language. They grasp analogies that older, more experienced minds reject as absurd. In intellectual development they move from the imaginative and pre-logical toward discursive, reasoned forms of thought. If we impose alien structures too soon—expecting children to read and write expository forms foreign to them—we invite failure and disinterest.

Scholars like Ernst Cassirer, Edward Sapir, and Otto Jesper-son have confirmed that the essence of language is not communi-cation. The egocentric speech of children is one indication that the purely communicative aspect of language has been exagger-ated. Language in the young, who as they begin to learn language babble both to learn and for the sheer joy of the sound, is as likely to be expressive as utilitarian. Children delight in the repetition of words and phrases for their sound, even when their meaning eludes the youngsters. The affective aspect of language, sorely neglected in formal education, deserves primacy in the literary education of children.

Some years ago a film told the story of Victor, an adolescent captured in 1799 in southern France, where for years he had roamed like an animal, savage and mute. A young Doctor Itard undertook the boy's education. Acting on the assumption that language is produced primarily to serve practical ends, he strug-gled to teach Victor to communicate efficiently. The project was eventually abandoned and judged unsuccessful for a number of reasons. Among them was Dr. Itard's failure to realize how Victor used language. The child, for example, never used the word *lait* to obtain milk but only to express his pleasure after the en-joyment of it. Indeed, the few words Victor did master were spoken only when he contemplated their objects with joy or sorrow, not when he lacked anything.

Our advanced society places great value on the practical, pro-saic, discursive mode of language and thought. We begin to believe that language began as a utility, that metaphoric expres-sion is mere decoration or distortion of fact. Children are not so easily misled. With their natural affinity for the poetic, they thrive on poetic language. The prose route to literacy is a rough one, as teachers will testify who have to listen to pedestrian basal-reader prose haltingly read and peruse prose offerings that are like essays in a foreign language imperfectly learned.

Language is absorbed from top to toe, not by the head alone. Sylvia Ashton-Warner, in her celebrated efforts to help Maori children toward literacy, discovered the significance to children of the affective aspects of language. In her classic "textbook," *Teacher* (1965, p. 30), she writes:

> First words must have intense meaning for a child. . . . They must be part of his being. How much hangs on the love of reading, the instinctive inclination to hold a book. INSTINCTIVE. That's what it must be. . . . Words must be organically born from the dynamic life itself. (p. 30)

For Sylvia Ashton-Warner's pupils, written expression in the words of their personal "key" vocabularies was stimulated by dancing, because their teacher understood the basic relationship of the two rhythms. In children, language is as basic and rhythmic as their body language and as inextricably bound to it, but—perversely—in school we chain them to seats and insist that they use only their minds in growing literate.

Two teachers, of first and fifth grades, designed simple 12-week studies to interest their children in poetry (Fitzgerald, 1986; Horrocks, 1986). The treatment consisted of reading aloud for 10 minutes a day selections by critically acclaimed children's poets. Guided by Ann Terry's (1974) research into children's poetry preferences, the teachers emphasized narrative and humorous poems and those with strong patterns of rhythm and rhyme.

The teachers asked no questions after the readings, although they encouraged the children to comment and question. By the end of the first month, children were bringing poems they had discovered on their own to share with the class. Questionnaires administered before and after the studies included this item:

> I check out books of poetry from the library.
>   Never   Occasionally   Often

At the beginning of the studies, 3% of the fifth graders and 1% of the second graders checked "Often." At the end of the 12 weeks of the studies, this response was checked off by 60% of the fifth graders and 58% of the first graders. The questionnaires indicated, for both classes, a marked change in attitude toward poetry. Before the treatment, more than 60% of both classes perceived

poetry as "boring" or "difficult"; after the treatment, more than 75%
described it as "interesting" and "easy to understand." In both cases,
poetry writing, much of it undertaken independently, was an outgrowth of listening to quantities of verse.

Far from being an unnecessary frill, poetry is essential to the
development of genuine literacy. For the elementary school child,
it is important to note, this means the aesthetic experience of
poetry, not premature analysis and explication of it. Poems chosen for presentation to children should be at the children's level
of interest and understanding.

Experiencing poetry by listening to it, reading it aloud, chanting it, and moving to its rhythms are prerequisite activities for
later, formal studies. Children who experience an early, pleasurable exposure to quantities of fine poetry and verse are less likely,
as students in high school and college, to experience difficulties
with poetic conventions: its compactness; its use of simile, metaphor, and personification; its employment of assonance, ambiguity, and pun.

To begin where children are, then, is to begin with verse, to
capitalize on their nature and their natural proclivities. Phyllis
Rogovin (1985), a teacher-researcher who collected examples of
poetic devices in children's speech, comments:

> Knowing that children enjoy using poetic devices when they
> relax and play, it is safe to assume that if they were carefully
> exposed to poetry, they could appreciate it as much as, if not
> more than any other form of literature. Daily doses of rhyth-
> mic and rhyming poems, similar to the patterns already famil-
> iar to them in the street, would be the starting point to capture
> their interest and imagination. I have found that poems like
> David McCord's "Pickety Fence" [1974, p. 7] do just that. (p. 3)

BRINGING CHILDREN AND POETRY TOGETHER

Choice of Poems

There is one rule of thumb for the choice of poetry to be used
with children: It should be the best available. It is essential that
it be "poetic" in the sense of being imagistic and rhythmic. Good
poems employ metaphor and image effectively and delightfully;

they have strong sensory appeal; many illustrate patterns of repe-
.tition and rhyme. Poems chosen for use with children should
speak to them at their level of understanding, but they ought also
to stretch minds and imaginations with fresh insights, novel ways
of seeing the world, and unusual but apt ways with words.

Riddles, good examples of metaphoric imagery, belong in a
central place at every grade level in the elementary school. In
riddles and conundrums, rhymed or unrhymed, the poet's way
of looking at the world is clearly evident; analogy and association are used with telling effect. Early experience with epigram-
matic sayings, concise and compact like proverbs, helps the child
to understand the economy inherent in poetic expression. Many
proverbs and epigrams are highly imagistic or metaphoric, illustrating at once two primary qualities of poetry.

Although it is the teachers' responsibility to bring the best of
poetry to children, they are choosing for children and therefore
need to read and listen to poems as a child would read and listen.
What delights a child may seem simplistic to an adult, but delight
is an important ingredient in poetry programs for children. The
wise teacher is one who learns from the pupils, encouraging them
to share their own favorites, whether from an anthology or from
the oral lore of childhood: jingles, chants, game-songs, taunt-songs,
word games, even the lively singing commercials learned from
television and radio or lyrics of pop songs. Choosing poetry to use
with children can never become an academic exercise.

Poems may be rhymed or unrhymed; they may be stories or
lyrics; they may be old or new; they may be on any subject that
might interest the children. Teacher-researchers have found
that children of all ages prefer humor and nonsense in poetry,
poems that tell stories and poems that rhyme (Fitzgerald, 1986;
Horrocks, 1986).

For foolproof introductions to poetry, choose works suitable
for children by major poets like

William Blake	Christina Rossetti
Emily Dickinson	Carl Sandburg
Robert Frost	Walt Whitman
Gerard Manley Hopkins	

Also recommended are contemporary writers of verse for children such as

Arnold Adoff
Dorothy Aldis
Harry Behn
N. M. Bodecker
John Ciardi
Walter de la Mare
Eleanor Farjeon
Aileen Fisher
Paul Fleischman
Nikki Giovanni
Eloise Greenfield
Langston Hughes
Leland Jacobs
X. J. Kennedy

Karla Kuskin
Dennis Lee
Myra Cohn Livingston
David McCord
Eve Merriam
A. A. Milne
Lilian Moore
Ogden Nash
Jack Prelutsky
James Reeves
Laura E. Richards
Shel Silverstein
Robert Louis Stevenson
Nancy Willard

Poetry as a Part of Daily Experience

Poetry cannot be relegated to an occasional lesson in its appreciation. As Leland Jacobs, educator and writer of children's verse, emphasizes in his lectures to teachers, it must become an integral part of daily living, embedded in the ritual of the classroom. Effective teachers will have poems on the tips of their tongues for all occasions: If someone has new shoes, a new baby brother, or a case of the sniffles; if an early robin appears, or the first flake of snow, they will be ready at a moment's notice with an appropriate poem or know where to find one to read aloud. Teachers are advised to develop personal collections of poems, to read from and for their students to browse in. A personal anthology is a ready resource when poems are needed at a moment's notice.

Ways must be found to bring poetry naturally and regularly into the classroom. It helps to encourage the children to develop personal anthologies of their own, as well as classroom anthologies containing class favorites. Anthologies may be written or tape-recorded or both. Festivals of poetry reading may be organized, with readers taking their favorites "on the road" to share with other classes. Children in one class I know have a "gift of words" for every visitor to their classroom: Favorite poems—the children's own or those of published poets—are copied carefully by the students, the papers rolled and tied with colored yarn, and arranged in a basket for visitors to select from. One first-grade classroom I visited had poems displayed on large poetry posters, lettered and illustrated by the children.

Many teachers find the unit an effective way to bring substance and coherence to poetry presentations. Units may be developed by focusing on the works of one poet; by comparing or contrasting the works of two or more; by concentrating for a time on a type of poetry like the ballad, limerick, sonnet, and the like; by reading and listening to poems on one topic or subject; by searching for poems that relate to material being studied in mathematics, social studies, or science. This last activity is especially useful in showing children that poetic insights are possible for all subjects, including those—like science and mathematics—typically talked about in discursive language.

The Importance of Oral Presentation

Poet Eve Merriam is a recipient of the National Council of Teachers of English Award for Excellence in Poetry for Children. *Out Loud* (Merriam, 1974) is both the title of a volume of her verse and also her poetry-presentation philosophy in two words. "If we can get teachers to read poetry, lots of it, out loud to children, we'll develop a generation of poetry lovers; we may even have some poetry writers. But the main thing, we'll have language appreciators" (Sloan, 1981, p. 960).

In the elementary school years, and even before formal education begins, children should experience poetry orally. Students develop an antipathy toward poetry only after they become independent readers, when there is a great possibility that poetry will become for them nothing more than static rows of print on a page, perhaps the subject of analysis and dissection, or something that they must memorize under pressure. The silent treatment of poetry can never result, at least for the young child, in an appreciation and enjoyment of poetry. Poetry should be read aloud, as effectively as possible, by the teacher, who in most cases will be the best oral interpreter the child will encounter. Recordings may be used for variety, but they are never a substitute for the live performance that involves direct sharing between a teacher and a class. Children should be encouraged but not coerced to read aloud to others, with preparation always preceding performance. All oral interpreters ought to prepare their presentations, selecting only those poems that they most enjoy, for these will be the best read.

Artistic responses to poetry (and other forms of imaginative literature) are particularly appropriate. Responding through art respects the aesthetic experience and extends it. Affective response is often intense and complicated, difficult if not impossible to put into words. Through nonlineal and multidimensional artistic responses students can come closer to an expression of their personal aesthetic experiences. The creation of visual art in response to poetry (and story) may take many forms. Janice Dressel (1988) describes how students created collages of words and pictures taken from magazines to express their response to and interpretation of literary works they had experienced. Using paint, clay models, or constructions of various kinds, students may visually render the personal meaning and significance to them of a literary work of art. In these renderings, children are encouraged to strive for a personal and interpretive creation rather than one that is simply literal or representational.

As often as possible, the oral experience with poetry ought to be accompanied with a physical response. Children should repeat lines and verses that have natural appeal, perhaps joining in on the refrain as they listen to a verse such as

> A farmer went trotting upon his grey mare,
>   Bumpety, bumpety, bump!
> With his daughter behind him so rosy and fair,
>   Lumpety, lumpety, lump!
>
> A raven cried, Croak! and they all tumbled down,
>   Bumpety, bumpety, bump!
> The mare broke her kees and the farmer his crown,
>   Lumpety, lumpety, lump!
>
> The mischievous raven flew laughing away,
>   Bumpety, bumpety, bump!
> And vowed he would serve them the same the next day,
>   Lumpety, lumpety, lump!

Moving to the rhythms of the poem is to be encouraged. It is natural for little children to gallop to "Ride a cock horse," walk with "To market, to market," march smartly to "The Grand Old Duke of York," or hop in time with A. A. Milne's (1924) "Hoppity" (p. 10).

Poems may be acted out as well as moved to, their rhythmic qualities brought to life through physical response. For older children it is fun to act out the action words of a poem: "slink," "dance," "creep," "rush," and the like. The acting may be representational, with children taking turns miming each episode of, say, A. A. Milne's (1924) "The King's Breakfast" (p. 64) or "The Highwayman" by Alfred Noyes (1902), while others read the poem aloud.

Avoid Verse Vivisection

This is the advice of Leland Jacobs, a militant against the misuse of poetry in classrooms. Poems must be respected and enjoyed for what they are—imaginative constructs that are not translatable into utilitarian prose. No effort should be made to extract what is often erroneously called a poem's "real" meaning.

The question, "What does it mean?" has no place in the study of poetry at any level, because it fails to make a necessary distinction between imaginative and discursive writing. Trying to translate a poem into discursive commentary is a fruitless and wasteful procedure. The effort confuses children, giving them the erroneous impression that poetry exists only as a distortion of prose. Instead, the child should be helped to know, by means of the best examples and with enjoyment and experimentation, that poetry is a valid mode of thought.

Students in Leland Jacobs' children's literature classes at Teachers College, Columbia University, were treated to a telling example of how the experience of a poem may be twice ruined: by overteaching it and by treating it as discourse. Professor Jacobs recited "The Goblin" to classes of teachers and mimicked the absurdity of misguided teachers who would ask of a poem to be enjoyed solely for its sounds and rhythm such questions as "What does it mean?" "Where, children, does the goblin live?" "How many things does he do?" "Can you name each one in its proper order?"

THE GOBLIN

A goblin lives in *our* house, in *our* house, in *our* house,
A goblin lives in *our* house all the year round.
He bumps
And he jumps
And he thumps
And he stumps.
He knocks
And he rocks

And he rattles at the locks.
A goblin lives in *our* house, in *our* house, in *our* house,
A goblin lives in *our* house all the year round.

Rose Fyleman

If a poem requires considerable explication and commentary
by the teacher before, during, or after the reading of it, it is probably the wrong choice for a particular group. Poems should stand
by themselves, requiring few if any props, at eye level with children. Occasionally it may be necessary to clarify a concept or offer
the meaning of a word before reading a poem to a class but, in
general, even this practice should be avoided. A better plan is to
encourage the children's own questions about points that bewil-
der or intrigue. In giving children freedom to experience poetry,
teachers need to be listeners as students comment on how a poem
affected them. In this early stage of criticism, experience of the
poem is the best teacher.

The emphasis is always on delight rather than dissection. In
Archibald MacLeish's words, "A poem should not mean but be."
"It takes children a long time," say the Opies, "before they cease
to be amazed that one word can have more than one meaning"
(1959, p. 31). Certainly a literary education worthy of the name
should see to it that this amazement with the delightful things
that words can do is fostered and made to last a lifetime.

This can never be accomplished through unpalatable practices such as vivisection. Children's initial experiences with
poetry must center in delight. Only if this is so are more analyti-
cal procedures possible and palatable as the child grows older.
And even these must be planned to enhance and not destroy the
essence of the poetic experience.

Experience of poetry, as with story, is the first step in criticism at the elementary and middle school level. A personal
response—verbal, physical, artistic—to the aesthetic experience
is the preferred first critical act for young students. The poems
themselves are the instructors, showing children what witty and
wonderful things words can be made to do.

7

Developing a Sense of Story

A Student: "Who is this Stecher? [a character created by William Carlos Williams]. . . . He's a mass of words, I suppose . . .
but, oh, now, part of me! . . . I picture him and can hear him talking. And he looks different to each one of us. . . . He's inside
us. . . . I can see him walking, or working. . . . Williams' words
have become my images and sounds, part of me. You don't do
that with theories. You don't do that with a system of ideas. You
do it with a story, because in a story—oh, like it says in the Bible,
The word becomes flesh."

—Robert Coles (1989, p. 128)

The importance of story in human lives goes well beyond literacy. Experience and intuition tell us this, and the knowledge is
confirmed in the work of narratologists, students of narrative and
of its significance in our lives (Culler, 1978). "Given the least
prompting, we are disposed to arrange around people and things
a meaningful sequence of events" (Rosen, 1985, p. 7; 1986). We
recognize the truth in Barbara Hardy's (1977) famous discussion
of narrative.

My argument is that narrative, like lyric and dance, is not to
be regarded as an aesthetic invention used by artists to control, manipulate, and order experience, but as a primary act of
mind transferred to art from life. . . . What concerns me are the
qualities which fictional narrative shares with that inner and
outer storytelling that plays a major role in our sleeping and
waking lives. For we dream in narrative, remember, anticipate,
hope, despair, believe, doubt, plan, revise, criticize, construct,

gossip, learn, hate, and love by narrative. In order really to live, we make up stories about ourselves and others, about the personal as well as the social past and future. (p. 12)

THE HUMAN NEED FOR STORY

In *The Uses of Enchantment,* Bruno Bettelheim (1976) discusses the importance of story to our psychological development. Through story, especially the fantasy of fairytales, Bettelheim argues, we are offered a way to articulate and explore our view of the world—a safe, objective means of making "some coherent sense out of the turmoil of . . . feelings" (p. 24).

A child's "sense of story"—a gradually evolving awareness of story form—is both a literary understanding and a facet of general development. The objective spectator stance that story allows us to bring to experience provides us with the means "to articulate and explore our view of the world, presenting alternatives, clarifying dark corners, posing contradictions, reconciling conflicts within the realm of our subjective, personal experience" (Applebee, 1978, p. 134). Stories are read more with the imagination and the emotions than with the reason. They are not judged against external standards of truth and logic, as are informational pieces. People who know the ways of stories do not ask: Is there a Yellow Brick Road? Although it may not be found on a road map, they understand that it exists as an imaginative reality. Those who have had plenty of experience with story are ready and willing to suspend disbelief and accept a story's postulates. The realization—which comes through the experience of imaginative literature—that many unusual premises are imaginatively conceivable widens personal perspectives and opens one to a greater range of possibilities in thought and action.

In terms of literacy, as a child's sense of story form and convention develops, it becomes an internalized representation, a schema, which aids comprehension. Listening to quantities of stories is the best preparation for reading them independently. Immersion in stories is essential to the growth of a child's sense of what stories are and how they are made: their patterns, language, and the conventions generally associated with this literary form. This sense improves the readers' ability in predicting syntax and meaning and in reading comprehension in general (Meek, 1982; Smith, 1983; Wells, 1986). Not surprisingly, a gradually evolving awareness of story form manifests itself in stylistic richness and complexity in children's speaking and writing (Eckhoff, 1983; Fox, 1983; Hickman, 1986).

Stories exert a strong motivational pull on readers and listeners. Moved by a story that excites or delights, children are likely to want to read on their own. Simply experiencing stories as works of art, savoring reactions and responses to them—reveling in the aesthetic experience—is of first importance in the development of literacy. Northrop Frye (1963a) said that an essential aspect of literary training is the art of listening to stories, which—far from being a passive act—is what he calls "a basic training for the imagination" (p. 43).

For both psychological and linguistic reasons, listening to and reading stories are essentials in the child's development. Stories teach children to read and write. Stories help children to make sense of their inner and outer worlds. Stories convince them that reading is worth doing.

EXPERIENCING LITERATURE: A CRITIC'S FIRST STEP

Experiencing literature is the first step in the study of it. Children can't talk about what they haven't experienced, nor can they make connections among works of literature unless they are well-read. Through television, comics, series books, and movies, most children are well-educated in the literary subculture. What they are likely to lack, and therefore what school must provide, is the experience of the best from among a wide variety of children's literature, old and new.

The experience of literature and certainly the study of it are often reserved for superior readers and reasoners. If children are slow learners or if English is a second language for them, common belief has it that they have time in school only to pursue utilitarian communication skills. This elitist approach to literary studies is nonsense, not to mention antihumanistic. Like all other children, the less intellectually gifted child or the child who has minimal English deserves literature (Heath, 1985; Rigg & Allen, 1989; Spack, 1985). To develop as critics, children must experience quantities of stories—and poems, of course, as discussed separately in Chapter 6. For some children, this experience may come at first only through listening.

Listening to Stories

Children understand with the ear what may be beyond them as independent readers. Reading aloud to all children, whether they can read for themselves or not, is a must for every classroom. There are numerous compelling reasons why.

First, there is the mutual pleasure that comes with reading to someone. At storytime, there are moments of true communion between children and an adult. Reading for no other purpose than shared enjoyment places much-needed emphasis on the aesthetics of reading, emphasis that is neglected in the relentless pursuit of main ideas and significant details in directed reading lessons.

I cherish memories of laughter and tears shared with children I've taught. At a reunion in the school where I taught in the 1950s, a man who had been in one of my third-grade classes said, "I remember how you always read to us; you made a reader of me."

Second, as my former third grader suggests, there is a motivational aspect in hearing books read. The very enjoyment they experience as listeners convinces children that reading is worth doing. Hearing a story interpreted by a competent, enthusiastic reader not only gives children pleasure, but the experience also brings a sense of what proficient reading can be like. For learners whose own reading may falter, this is essential modeling. Reading aloud assigns a special role to reading, signalling to the child that adults find reading worthwhile and enjoyable. Further, an oral presentation allows listeners to hear the storyteller's voice. Carefully crafted prose, like poetry, is meant to be heard; in imaginative literature especially, words are chosen for their rhythm and sound as well as their sense.

Third, regularly hearing quantities of fine stories read aloud significantly improves children's vocabulary and reading comprehension, and results in greater complexity and sophistication of syntax in both oral and written language (Meek, 1982). For learners of English, hearing the cadences of the language is of inestimable value in developing reading facility (Rigg & Allen, 1989).

A teacher need not be the only oral reader in a classroom. Children can read to partners, with benefits accruing on both sides. Older children can prepare picture books to read to children in lower grades. Some schools encourage adult volunteers to serve as reading partners in classrooms.

Selecting Stories to Read Aloud

Children ought to experience the widest possible variety of stories: myths, Bible tales told as stories, folktales and fairytales, tales of the heroes of epic and romance, fables, stories of contemporary life, modern fantasy, and all the rest. Most stories for children are in either the comic or romantic modes, but stories in the tragic and ironic-satiric modes or stories with elements of these modes are now written for children and need to be included with the other two types to ensure exposure to the full circle of story types. To know only romantic and comic structures is not to advance beyond childlike tastes, with subsequent problems in appreciating "heavier" stories like the Shakespearean tragedies encountered in high school.

Myths, Bible stories, fairytales, and legends are central to the critical process, because this traditional literature is to later literary works what still life is to painting: studies in form. Through experience with traditional forms of story, children not only internalize a sense of the structure of all storytelling, but also develop a potential critical standard, essential in a world of subliterary entertainment.

A knowledge of myth and legend, Bible stories, and ancient epics is essential to one's full appreciation of later literature with its countless allusions to the traditional stories. Deprived of the sources of allusion, the reader is like someone limited in mathematics through lack of knowledge of the multiplication tables.

The traditional stories of a culture put children in contact with many of the social myths that have figured in the development of their society. Every society has a central group of stories that inform not only its literature but other aspects of its social life as well. Literary works that express informing social myths are not invariably works of great literary distinction, but they are of interest nonetheless. In America, these stories often present a nostalgic vision of the country's early history and feature cowboys, pioneers, hunters, and self-made tycoons, together with biographical tales of mythologized heroes like Washington and Franklin.

The interests and developmental level of a particular group of children are the first considerations in selecting material to read to children. However, as professionals aware of the needs of a particular class, teachers will select some reading materials that match the children's interests and other materials that will spark new interests and broaden literary experience. For older children who have not encountered much of it, the wonders of modern fantasy—works by Lloyd Alexander, Ursula K. Le Guin, Madeleine L'Engle, Robin McKinley, to name a few outstanding authors in the genre—can be an exciting revelation. Stories that children might not attempt on their own or comprehend if they did—the classics like *Tom Sawyer*, for example, with their many pages and often unfamiliar vocabulary—are among the best choices for oral reading to groups. Biographies and historical fiction are sometimes dismissed by children as difficult or dull. The reading aloud of one or two of the best of these—by writers like Jean Fritz, Kathryn Lasky, Jean Little, and Milton Meltzer—will go far in correcting this misconception.

Literary excellence is another primary consideration in selection: Important themes, memorable language, well-drawn characters, plots with streamlined structures, complementary text and illustrations, and fresh, innovative treatment of a subject are among the criteria to be considered. The stories need to be well beyond mediocre, far past the trivial tales that merely mirror experience without examining its paradox, intricacy, and ambiguity. The less challenging literature is more accessible—because of its ubiquity and simplicity—and children are likely to come to it on their own. Most books we read aloud, whether humorous or serious, ought to give listeners a thing or two to wonder about, marvel at, and talk about. Among the contemporary authors who write books for older children are

Byrd Baylor	Gary Paulsen
Natalie Babbitt	Richard Peck
Lucille Clifton	Cynthia Rylant
Paula Fox	Ouida Sebestyen
Virginia Hamilton	Elizabeth Speare
Florence Heide	Mildred Taylor
Lois Lowry	Cynthia Voight
Patricia MacLachlan	E. B. White
Nicolasa Mohr	Laurence Yep
Walter Dean Myers	Jane Yolen
Katherine Paterson	

Children of preschool and primary grade age are particularly responsive to stories featuring repetitive patterns and refrains, as in the enduring *Millions of Cats* (Gag, 1928) and *Caps for Sale*

(Slobodkina, 1947) or in inspired retellings of favorite folktales such as *Chicken Little* by Steven Kellogg (1985) or Paul O. Zelinsky's *Rumpelstiltskin* (1986). Not only do the children enjoy predictable books, but research also shows that their predictability facilitates learning to read and comprehending what is read (Baghban, 1984).

Some authors who write for young children and use memorable language to tell engrossing stories—with and without repetitive patterns—are

Anthony Browne	Arnold Lobel
Miriam Cohen	Amy Schwartz
Pat Cummings	Maurice Sendak
Tomie DePaola	Marjorie Sharmat
Roger Duvoisin	William Steig
Russell Hoban	Rosemary Wells
Pat Hutchins	Charlotte Zolotow

In studies of children's preferences in upper elementary grades and middle school, teacher-researchers found that fast-paced stories featuring strong characters in humorous or perilous situations had the strongest appeal (Sloan, 1988). They discovered also that, with practice, listeners can appreciate more leisurely, reflective writing. In one study lasting 15 weeks, a class of fifth graders began by listening to simpler books of less than 100 pages and ended able to listen attentively to the complex fantasies of Susan Cooper, Ursula K. Le Guin, and Lloyd Alexander.

Although teachers on occasion may, for various reasons, judiciously cut bits from the texts they read aloud, abridged or simplified versions of works must be avoided. An author's style is in the language the author used. When the language is altered, the integrity of the piece is lost. Edited versions or insipid retellings, where language is simplified, are little more than summaries. The best translations, the finest versions of old tales, or the most masterly contemporary retellings of them must be sought. (Excellent bibliographies of recommended versions may be found in *The Riverside Anthology of Children's Literature* [Saltman, 1985] and similar anthologies. See also Resources for Teachers at the back of the book.) The unique style of storytellers like Rudyard Kipling needs to be heard in the original. In Kipling's *Just-so Stories* (1902/ 1987), for example, the outrageous flights of fancy are related in this storyteller's singular voice and they must be read "just so."

In the beginning of years, when the world was new and all, and
the Animals were just beginning to work for Man, there was a
Camel, and he lived in the middle of a howling Desert because
he did not want to work; and besides, he was a Howler himself. So he ate sticks and thorns and tamarisks and milkweed
and prickles, most 'scruciating idle; and when anybody spoke
to him he said "Humph!" Just "Humph!" and no more. (p. 139)

THE CLASSROOM INDEPENDENT READING PROGRAM:
WHY AND HOW

Listening to stories—and poems, as discussed in Chapter 6—
is essential in a literary education. So is the independent reading
of genuine texts, most of them stories. My reasons for emphasizing stories in the individualized or independent reading program
are discussed earlier in this chapter. The conventional, predictable structures of stories, when readers are familiar with them,
help to make these printed texts comprehensible. Stories are read
primarily for enjoyment, for affect, for an aesthetic experiencing.
Certainly on a first reading, readers needn't struggle to remember facts and details to take beyond the initial experience, as they
often must do when they study informational material. Stories
have a mysterious hold on most of us; few people of any age can
resist the pull of a good story. Independent reading is not part of
a directed reading lesson. It is time for the application of the skills
learned in directed reading lessons, for individual exploration and
experimentation, and most of all for enjoyment.

Many reading programs in elementary and middle schools
deal almost entirely with how to read, even though we are far from
being certain exactly how reading is accomplished. We do know
that reading is a skill that is developed by actually practicing it
with genuine reading materials and not by filling workbooks with
exercises that relate peripherally to it. That is why an independent reading component is absolutely essential in all literacy
programs.

Every effective reading program has three components: directed reading lessons, skill-building exercises—*as required by
individuals*—and a regular in-school program of independent
reading. Directed reading lessons may use a variety of materials:
basal reader selections, passages from science or social studies
texts, newspaper articles, novels, and stories. In many literature-

based literacy programs, literature—stories and poems—is used for directed reading lessons. This is entirely acceptable, providing that the literary works are treated as works of art and not as informational pieces. However, directed reading lessons, whatever their content, cannot be considered the whole reading program.

At least half the time allotted for reading in school should be spent in individualized or independent reading, defined as reading, for enjoyment or enlightenment, material—with emphasis on imaginative literature—that children choose for themselves. This, it should be noted, is a straightforward, simple procedure that requires no kits, manuals, or complex doctrine for its implementation. There is no guru of independent reading, unless Jeanette Veatch, Professor Emerita of Arizona State University, might be called one. Her little book, *How to Teach Reading with Children's Books* (Veatch, 1968), is a study in simplicity and sound advice that takes the mystery out of teaching with children's literature. Many of its ideas are incorporated into the following suggestions for the implementation of an independent or individualized component of the reading program—which I have personally and through my students tested in classrooms, grades 1 through 9.

Acquiring the Books

An independent reading program centers on books and time in school to read them. Since it is advisable to keep a classroom book collection from becoming static, a good plan is to borrow books from the school or public library for several weeks at a time. Librarians offer invaluable help in selecting books tailored to the needs and interests of a group of children.

Library books may be supplemented with donations from the children themselves, dividend books from class membership in book clubs, or gleanings from garage and library sales.

Two to three books per child is generally considered the optimum size for the classroom library, with books ranging in difficulty from easy to challenging. The classroom collection, chosen with the children's interests and ability levels in mind, should consist mainly of stories at the elementary and middle school levels, including biographies and historical fiction. Volumes of poetry and plays also belong in the collection. A suitable classroom library reflects the developmental needs and the interests of a particular class and is not viable unless these are taken into consideration.

For a class of older, resistant readers, in which several spoke English as a second language and many had never read a book in its entirety, the teacher prepared a selection of "mini-books," manila folders holding short pieces chosen to interest her group of aliterates: magazine articles, editorials, the occasional poem, works of short fiction. Another teacher of a similar group included in the classroom library picture books whose content made them acceptable to older students, among them *The Last Free Bird* (Stone, 1967), *Crow Boy* (Yashima, 1976), *Mufaro's Beautiful Daughters* (Steptoe, 1987), *Sleeping Ugly* (Yolen, 1984), and *Jumanji* (Van Allsburg, 1981).

Thousands of books are published each year; thousands go out of print. Through a close association with children's librarians, teachers have access to lists of recent publications, reissues in paperback, award-winning books, and titles of the books children actually check out of the library.

Most teachers enjoy the research necessary for selecting books for their classes. Ours is a golden age of children's literature. The finest contemporary artists have illustrated distinguished picture books. A selective list of these artists follows:

Aliki
Verna Aardema
Molly Bang
Marcia Brown
Eric Carle
Barbara Cooney
Pat Cunningham
Diane and Leo Dillon
Roger Duvoisin
Tom Feelings
Ann Grifalconi
Gail E. Haley
Syd Hoff
Nonny Hogrogian
Pat Hutchins
Trina Schart Hyman
Ezra Jack Keats
Steven Kellogg
Jack Kent
Karla Kuskin

Leo Lionni
Arnold Lobel
David Macaulay
Mercer Mayer
Robert McCloskey
Gerald McDermott
Barry Moser
Helen Oxenbury
Peter Parnall
Jerry Pinkney
Alice Provensen
Martin Provensen
Robert Quackenbush
Maurice Sendak
Nancy Tafuri
Chris Van Allsburg
Rosemary Wells
Ed Young
Margot Zemach

Dozens of writers whose books are catalogued as youth literature are admired by adults who get to know their work. In addition to those authors cited earlier in the chapter, the following
are notable writers for older readers:

Joan Aiken	Jane Langton
Bruce Brooks	Madeleine L'Engle
Hester Burton	Jean Little
Leon Garfield	Anne McCaffrey
Mollie Hunter	Scott O'Dell
Diana Wynne Jones	Philippa Pearce
M. E. Kerr	Zilpha Snyder
E. L. Konigsburg	Ivan Southall

A Place for Nonfiction

In choosing books for children, I have given the highest prior-
ity to works of the imagination: poems and stories. However,
through wide reading in children's literature, it becomes obvious
that the line between fiction and nonfiction is often blurred (Carr,
1982, 1987; Crook & Lehman, 1991). This is particularly evident
in biographies. It is also true of books which, although they do
not tell a story in the traditional format of characters coping
through a definite sequence of beginning, middle, and end, do
make a vivid appeal to the child's imagination and sense of wonder. The nonfiction works of skilled, sensitive creative artists may
indeed be considered within the categories of poems and stories
as part of children's total literary experience. Such works ought
to be included in classroom libraries and in units of study.
    In the nonfiction works of Aliki, Tomie DePaola, Lois Ehlert,
Russell Freedman, Gail Gibbons, Joe Lasker, Kathryn Lasky,
David Macaulay, Bruce Macmillan, Milton Meltzer, Gary Paulsen,
Glen Rounds, and Cynthia Rylant—to name a few outstanding
artists in the genre—are embodied the characteristics of fine fiction and poetry: rhythmic pacing; suspense; memorable, metaphorical language; and a sense of wonder in the mysteries and
ambiguities inherent in all aspects of life on the planet.
    The melding of the factual and the poetic is often experienced
to the greatest extent through the medium of the picture book.
One example is *The King's Day: Louis XIV of France* (Aliki, 1989),
where words and pictures combine to present an intriguing por-

trait of the Sun King's life. Others include *Chicka Chicka Boom Boom* (Martin & Archambault, 1989), a highly imaginative alphabet book in lively rhyme that tells a "story" of alphabet letters clambering to the top of a coconut tree, and *One Hungry Monster* (O'Keefe, 1989), a rhymed counting book that tells a rollicking tale of mayhem and mischief.

Patricia Lauber's *The News About Dinosaurs* (1989), an Orbis Pictus honor book (the NCTE Orbis Pictus Award is for outstanding nonfiction) is an example of this superb nonfiction writer's work in which material, presented where possible from a definitive point of view, is often organized in a suspenseful narrative.

Heartland (Siebert, 1989) movingly combines poetic text and magnificent paintings by Wendell Minor to spellbind as well as impart information about farming in the Midwest. The list of fine examples of such books is virtually limitless, as researchers will discover in their quest for the best books in all genres that will capture children's interests and ignite their imaginations.

Help in Finding the Best Books

For those who need guidance in choosing the finest books available for children, a good place to begin is with the Caldecott and Newbery award-winning and honor books (runners-up). The Randolph Caldecott medal, named for a nineteenth-century British illustrator of books for children, is awarded each year for the most distinguished picture book for children published in the United States. The John Newbery Medal, named for an eighteenth-century British publisher who was the first to publish books especially for children, is given annually for the most distinguished contribution to literature for children published in the United States. Selection of both awards is made by a committee of the American Library Association. Consult Resources for Teachers in this book for information on obtaining lists of winners of both awards since their inception and for other resources helpful in book selection and curriculum development.

Guided Reading of a Picture Book or Novel

A guided or directed reading of a picture book or novel is an effective way to launch an independent reading program. The oral presentation of a book (preferred in this case) or the silent reading by all students of the same book provides a common experience, which becomes the basis for discussion by the entire class or small groups within it. Some teachers find it good practice to start by modeling discussion techniques with the whole class. Prepared by a guided reading experience, independent readers proceed with greater confidence toward richer experiences with books they read on their own.

Study Stories as Entities.   Some procedures for directed reading—and other teacher-guided approaches to study—are recommended; others need to be avoided. For one thing, the story must be experienced as an aesthetic whole before it is "studied." This doesn't preclude the occasional stopping at a climactic point to ask students to predict what will happen next. Actually, prediction—asking about what students will read or hear—is a highly desirable strategy; it leads to more critical thinking than does questioning to recall bits and pieces of a story already read or heard. However, the story as an artistic whole always must be preserved.

Stories Are Fiction, Not Fact.   Another point must be kept in mind: Stories are imaginative constructs, not informational treatises or assemblages of facts. Stories go more for affect than fact. Therefore, the personal experience of a story is an important part of literary criticism. Interpretations of the text in the form of examples and illustrations from the student's own life represent a higher order of thinking than do factual answers drawn verbatim from the text. Students should approach an imaginative work more with the imagination than with reason.

Divergent and Convergent Thinking.   Consideration of a work centers on certain key words: imagining, theorizing, hypothesizing, evaluating, synthesizing. Divergent thinking, where a number of possibilities—about a character's motivation, say—are posed and tested, is valued. (Examples: What is going to happen now? What's another possibility?) So is convergent thinking, in which students must listen to each other, reflect on the story, and decide on the validity of interpretations resulting from divergent thinking. (Examples: Which prediction do you think is most accurate? Which of our predictions are still valid? No longer valid?) In talking about books, the aim is not to have a quiz in which there are right and wrong answers but to have a shared discussion of possible interpretations of a text. Ferreting out facts about the story is, of course, the opposite of this.

Common Elements in Story.   Each story is unique, yet the same elements are found in every story: characters; setting; point of view; language, including dialogue; plot, which contains conflict or problem, suspense, foreshadowing, climax, denouement; tone; and theme. The focus of a book discussion should be less on facts about a story's content and more on how these elements are combined to make meaning in the story. For this reason, specific questions on each book are often unnecessary; indeed, reams of questions after each chapter are a sure indication of overkill. It is usually better to base discussion on questions that apply to stories in general. In this approach a work is not dissected under a microscope. Instead, students step back from the work the better to see its shape and form; stepping even further back allows students to see works in relation to each other. The analogies and resemblances students find in all their literary experiences should be stressed in discussion.

Content in Terms of Form and Structure.   In developing questions to help children—directed or undirected—in the exploration of literary works, teachers need to think of the works in terms of their structure and form, not merely in terms of their content. Of course, in the discussion of literature, content cannot be ignored, However, it always can be considered in relation to the form and structure of a work. Characters often behave the way they do in order for a story to develop along certain lines; characters may, in fact, be examined structurally. For example, in *Charlotte's Web* (White, 1952), Templeton, an undesirable character, is probably not one children would choose to emulate or to have as a friend, but he serves the purpose of the plot precisely because he is undesirable. (These two rather pointless questions about characters encountered in a story are often asked of children: Would you do as X did? Would you like to have X as a friend?)

Each reader and listener brings to literature personal likes and dislikes that color and enrich each response. The content of literary works may challenge values and offer new and provocative possibilities for thinking about experience. While literature relates to each one's life experiences, these relations cannot be the basis for systematic criticism. Nor can a view of literature as purely content provide such a basis. Children need to be discouraged, as they undertake the stage of criticism beyond personal response, from considering works solely for messages, morals, key ideas, and miscellaneous general knowledge.

The Tale of Peter Rabbit (Potter, 1902), for example, may be seen as a moral tale. Read one way it teaches that if you disobey your mother, you may be endangered, lose your clothes, feel ill, and be sent to bed with medication. Another valid interpretation of the content is that disobedience can lead to excitement. In either case, the literary point of the story is lost. Without Peter's character and behavior there would be no story, for his tale is in the form of the romance, the adventurous quest, which requires a courageous hero to go forth, successfully complete a quest, and return home triumphant.

Examples of Questions

To assist teachers in conducting a guided reading experience, examples of questions that deal with story content in terms of form and structure are presented below. Note that these questions are not tied to one particular story but may be applied to stories in general. (Refer to Chapter 8 for further examples of questions to elicit discussion.) In leading book discussions, it is always wise to begin by listening closely to the initial free responses of the children and building upon them. For instance, if at the conclusion of a story a child says, "That's not a good ending" (a comment on plot), beginning discussion will center on plot, in this case probably with a question prefaced by "Why?"

Type of Story

• Every storyteller constructs a make-believe world that may be very like our own or entirely different from it. What signs and signals indicate whether a story will be more fanciful than realistic? (Talking animals; exaggeration; strange, improbable situations, characters, or settings; stories that begin: "Once upon a time. . . .")

• If the world created by the author is far different from the one we know, how does the author make the story seem possible and believable? (The author creates the world down to the last detail. For example, C. S. Lewis gives his magical land of Narnia a complete geography, with land forms, plants, and weather.)

Setting and Plot

• Where and when does the story take place? How do you know? If the story took place somewhere else or in a different time, how would it be changed? (Readers will recognize that specific time and place are less important to some stories than to others. In historical fiction like *One Is One* [Picard, 1966], the medieval setting is central to the story; *The Pushcart War* [Merrill, 1964] could take place in no city other than New York; exactly where *Konrad* [Nostlinger, 1977] takes place is less important than character and plot.)

• What incident, problem, conflict, or situation gets the story started? (Here readers and listeners focus on form, recognizing that a story begins at a particular point, usually with a conflict or an unresolved situation.)

• What is the basic shape of the story? (Successful quest—romance form; overcoming obstacles to some desired end—comic form; unfulfilled or partially fulfilled quest—irony-satire form; prevented in some way from reaching a desired end—tragic form. Younger students will readily understand these concepts through less technical terms: The quest pattern may be described as home-adventure-home, a circular story shape.)

• What does the author do to create suspense, to make you want to read on to find out what happens? Is what happens made credible and plausible? How? Did the author prepare you for what happens? How? (Suspense occurs because there is set up a situation that must be resolved; this resolution is delayed and detoured through dramatic scenes that deliberately delay and detour as they lead inevitably toward it. The author prepares you for what happens through foreshadowing but keeps you guessing as to the nature of the resolution. If the characters are made interesting and appealing enough, the reader wants to know their fate. Actions and events are made credible and plausible because they develop organically from the interplay of character and plot. There are no characters introduced only to serve the plot, no coincidences that make the plot seem contrived.)

• How is the story ordered for telling? (Chronological order; a series of episodes or incidents; flashbacks; told through letters or diary entries.)

• Trace the main events of the story. Is it possible to change their order? Leave any of them out? Why or why not? (A well-constructed story develops organically, action developing out of previous action with a sense of inevitability.)

• Suppose you thought of a different ending for the story. How would the rest of the story have to be changed to fit the new ending? (Consideration of this question helps readers to recognize unity in structure; a story is an organic whole, the ending inevitable, given its beginning and middle. Also considered here is character development in relation to incident.)

• Did the story end as you expected it to? What clues did the author offer to prepare you to expect this ending? Did you recognize these clues as important to the story as you first read or listened to it? Why are these clues important to your overall reaction to the story? (Clues, foreshadowings of what is to come, are often not apparent to inexperienced readers until the reading is complete. How subtly they are used is a mark of the author's skill and a structural aspect of story interesting to study. The plausibility of a story often hinges on the use of foreshadowing.)

Characters

• Who is the main character in the story? What kind of person is this character? How do you know? Do you sympathize with the character? Are you interested in the character's fate? Why? Can you figure out from the story why the characters behave as they do? Do you recognize here any character types that you know from other stories? (We learn about character through description, through the character's behavior, through what the character says and what others say about the character. Good writers reveal characters by showing dramatically what they are like rather than telling about them. Readers are meant to sympathize and identify with the main character of a story; when they do, because the character is like them or has a problem that interests them, they want to read on to find out how the character will fare. Writers need to let us know what motivates a character's actions. Motivation may be complex, but it should be believable.)

• Do any characters change in the course of the story? If so, how are they different in the end? What changed them? Does the change seem believable? (Readers see how, through incident and experience, characters change and develop; good storytellers make the change believable and inevitable. Some signs of a possible change are in the character from the beginning.)

• Some characters play small but important roles in a story. Pick out a bit player from a story. Why is this character necessary to the story? Do you recognize this character as similar to minor characters in other stories? (Minor characters act as foils, helping the reader to more clearly see a main character through contrast. Minor characters may be used to move a plot forward.)

Point of View

• Who tells the story? Is it told in first person—I? Is it the omniscient viewpoint of the all-knowing author, who uses third person—he, she, they? Is it limited omniscient point of view, where, although the story is told in third person, it concentrates on the thoughts and feelings of a central character? Is it the dramatic or objective point of view, which, like the camera, records action without comment? How does point of view affect tone, characterization, and credibility? (Young readers can begin to discuss the complex and fascinating question of point of view in stories. Some first-person novels feature young protagonists so precocious it is difficult to believe in them. First-person and limited omniscient viewpoints lend a sense of immediacy to the action; readers are one with the viewpoint character. However, the viewpoint is also limited to this one character.)

Mood or Tone

• Does the story as a whole create a definite mood or feeling? How is it created? Does the mood or tone change during the course of the story? How does the author signal this change? (Descriptions, particularly of settings, create mood; a lighthearted tone may be established through dialogue or when a character embarks on a trivial quest; a serious tone is set when a quest is serious. An author's language conveys tone and mood. The point of view used in a story influences tone and mood throughout. The imagery and symbolism used in a story establish tone and mood; certain patterns of imagery are associated with positive and negative experiences. For example, the harsh concrete world of the city sets the tone and mood for Walter Dean Myers' explorations of ghetto life.)

• Did you have strong feelings throughout the story? (Anger, hopelessness, fear, loathing, delight, joy, fear, sorrow, sympathy.)

• What did the author do to make you feel strongly? (Created sympathetic characters believably and set them in dramatic situations, making readers experience along with them and therefore care about what happens to them.)

Style

• Does the style of writing fit the subject? Do the characters speak naturally and in keeping with their setting? Is the language rich in imagery and in memorable ways of expressing ideas? Does it flow rhythmically when it is read aloud? (A casual contemporary style may not suit the substance of an ancient tale. Good writers have an ear for dialogue, letting us hear each character's distinctive voice. A good imaginative writer helps readers and listeners to visualize the action in clear detail. In a good book, language is used with flair to express unusual or telling insights.)

Theme

• What is the idea *behind* the story that gives point to the whole? (If a book leaves one thinking, "So what?" the theme is probably trivial or lacking altogether. Truly memorable literature examines the issues that concern people most: matters of love, loyalty, purpose in life, survival, courage, friendship, and the like. In a well-written story, thematic lessons are presented indirectly through the dramatic action, never preached or taught. Exploration of the informing ideas of a story is an important aspect of criticism and critical thinking; to do this exercise, children must analyze, synthesize, interpret, theorize, and hypothesize—all higher-order thinking skills.)

Making Connections

• Is this story, though different in content, like any other story you have read or watched in its form and structure? (A journey or quest; a struggle or predicament that is solved by magical intervention; a series of episodes of equal importance; the occurrence of magical change [metamorphosis]; a theme like good triumphing over evil; a motif like disguise; mistaken identity; or a pattern of three: trials, journeys, or wishes; a magical talisman; spells; curses.)

• Think of all the characters in the story. Are any of them the same or similar to characters in other stories, cartoons, comics, movies? (Brave hero or heroine, crafty villain, trickster, wise advisor, helpful friend, foolish one, underdog who wins against all odds, charming rogue, anti-hero or "loser," etc.)

Illustrations

Literary elements—plot, character, mood, tone, setting, and theme—are all present in picture books, and they may be studied through both text and pictures.

The size of characters, their place on the page and relation to setting and other characters, the choice and juxtaposition of images, the use of certain colors and lighting, all have literary significance.

While the cumulative rhyming text of *Drummer Hoff* (Emberley, 1967) tells the tale of the firing of a cannon, the right question will help children to discover how the final pictures reveal that the book as a whole carries a message of peace.

During an examination of *Mufaro's Beautiful Daughters* (Steptoe, 1987), children might consider why the artist chose always to picture Manyara in a harsh light. Young children will readily see how *Rosie's Walk* (Hutchins, 1968) is a study in suspense. They will recognize that the stylized pictures of Gerald McDermott's *The Stonecutter* (1975) enhance the mystery and wonder of a mythical tale.

ENCOURAGING WIDE READING

Getting children to read widely can be difficult. Youngsters are wary when it comes to both food and books, insisting that they don't like what they haven't even sampled. Children tend to prefer the familiar. Studies by teachers in my graduate classes showed that, in general, students left entirely to themselves to select their reading material were likely to always choose the same type of books. Moreover, most readers regularly chose books that offered little or no challenge in terms of readability.

One boy concentrated solely on sports fiction; other children in the 9-12 group read exclusively works of fiction depicting everyday life, like those of Judy Blume, Beverly Cleary, Carolyn Haywood, and Ellen Conford. Some children never read fiction at all; they simply leafed their way through informational books, looking at pictures. In every case, after a planned effort to introduce these children to challenging books that reflected their interests, all of them responded by reading more widely.

Interest Inventories

As part of their systematic efforts to encourage wider reading, teachers report success with interest inventories. Open-ended questions like the following were found to elicit the best response:

When I grow up, I want to _____
During my free time, I enjoy _____
Outside of school, my main interest is _____
The kind of story I like best is _____
If I wrote a book, it would be about _____

One teacher, discovering that a fifth-grade girl enjoyed riding, drew up for her a personalized list of fine horse stories that included classics such as *King of the Wind* (Henry, 1948), *The Black Stallion* (Farley, 1941), and *The Winged Colt of Casa Mia* (Byars, 1981b).

For a boy, an able reader in sixth grade, who revealed in his interest inventory that he liked stories from the twilight zone, another teacher prepared a list that included *The White Mountains* (Christopher, 1967), *The Eyes of the Amaryllis* (Babbitt, 1977), *The Ghost of Thomas Kempe* (Lively, 1973), and works by William Sleator, including *Interstellar Pig* (Sleator, 1984).

Responding to negative comments about reading in her batch of inventories ("I'd rather do anything than read" was the response of several students), one of my graduate students promised the resistant fourth graders books that were both funny and short. Her list, which helped to convert some nonreaders, included *Chocolate Fever* (Smith, 1972), *The Twenty-one Balloons* (DuBois, 1947), *Mr. Popper's Penguins* (Atwater, 1938), *Lizard Music* (Pinkwater, 1976), *Help! I'm a Prisoner in the Library*

(Clifford, 1981) and *The Dreadful Future of Blossom Culp* (Peck, 1983).

A teacher-librarian, realizing that too much time is wasted by children gazing at the spines of books on library shelves, provided them with lists based on the information gleaned from the interest inventories she administered. Among her lists were "Ten Top Authors of Mysteries," "Ten Golden Oldies," and "Ten to Make You Laugh Out Loud."

Oral Introductions to Books

Word-of-mouth is always the best advertising. When I taught in Toronto in the 1950s, we had no library in our old downtown school. Once a month, my third graders and I trekked along College Street to Boys and Girls House, the children's room of the Central Public Library. At the end of the journey, we were rewarded with book talks, the librarians introducing, by reading aloud enticing snippets of stories, a wide variety of books spanning a broad range of content and readability. Invariably, the books the librarians introduced—whether classic or contemporary, easy to read or not—were always those the children chose to carry back to school with them.

The power of advertising, in particular the personal testimonial, is awesome. One teacher initiated a campaign in her classroom to open the eyes of her sixth-grade realists to the glories of modern fantasy. She read widely herself, determined to advertise the genre with the best possible books. She selected to advertise such books as *The Owl Service* (Garner, 1968), *The Keeper of the Isis Light* (Hughes, 1981), *The Fledgling* (Langton, 1980), *A Wizard of Earthsea* (Le Guin, 1968), *Dr. Dread's Wagon of Wonders* (Brittain, 1987), and *A Darker Magic* (Bedard, 1987).

This teacher featured displays of these books in her classroom, but the main part of her advertising campaign was oral. As she read the books, she noted passages in them that were particularly tantalizing; these she read aloud when she gave book talks. She took time to create one-page scripts for Readers Theater, featuring passages of dialogue directly from the books, chosen to interest children in reading the entire book. Groups of students gave prepared readings of the scripts to the rest of the class. The teacher reported that, although her display included many more books than were presented through book talks and

Readers Theater performances, the books that she personally introduced were the ones the children clamored to read for themselves. Eventually, most of these sixth graders were reading fantasy, giving their own book talks, and preparing new scripts for Readers Theater.

Another teacher initiated The Sixty-Second Salestalk, in which her students had to "sell" to the class a book that they enjoyed. This lively method of reporting, the teacher found, was more effective by far than lists of books in persuading others to read. Students wanted to read what their classmates had read with enjoyment. In addition, the timed talks gradually, with practice, became better organized, more detailed, and more innovative.

RESPONSES TO INDEPENDENT READING

The Student–Teacher Conference

The conference is an essential part of the independent reading program. While it is usually a student-teacher conference, it need not be so exclusively. Parent volunteers, students from higher grades, and even classmates may conference with readers. Students need not conference after every book they read, although that option should be open to them. Holding a conference ought to be treated as a special time, an opportunity for students to share orally the experience of their book. Oral sharing of what one reads is a natural, pleasurable response to reading. During the conference—most last about 10 minutes—students should be encouraged to read aloud from their books a portion that had significance for them.

To hold a conference, teachers need not read the book. The child is the talker, the teacher the listener. Teachers soon discover, by careful listening, whether or not the child has read and comprehended the book. Quizzing children on the details they recall is to be avoided. Long drawn-out retellings of the plot are discouraged. Students need to understand that there are no "right" or "wrong" responses to a book. The teacher is interested in the students' opinions. Asking "Why?" after the following questions is a strategy that has been used with success by many teachers during conference time:

Did you finish the book?

What do you remember about the book?

What caught your interest most?

What pleased (or frightened, surprised, impressed, annoyed)
you?

Was this story like any other you've read or heard or seen?

Was there anything in the story that relates in some way to
you or your life?

Direct the child's attention to the form and structure of the
book.

What type of story was your book? (adventure? myth? legend? folk- or fairytale? mystery? science fiction? fantasy?
everyday experience? biography? historical fiction?)

Who tells this story?

Where and when does the story take place?

What problem or situation gets the story started?

Is the problem or situation solved by the end of the story?

Was it the ending you expected?

Was the working out of the story believable?

Is this story like any other you know?

Probe, using what the child has said: "You said that Joel's
friend drowns [in *On My Honor* (Bauer, 1986)] and Joel goes
home without telling anyone. Why do you think he did that?"
(Refer also to the procedures and questions previously discussed
in this chapter.)

The Child's Record Keeping

While there is no one formula or set procedure for a successful independent reading program, there is one emphatic negative: Do not assign formal, written book reports. These are the
kiss of death to motivation for reading.

In an independent reading program, reading is all-important.
What happens after the reading needs to be a natural, real-world
activity, not a school-type, reading-related activity. There are no
strings of questions to answer after a book is read. Record keeping for the children is kept simple. For example, titles and brief
evaluative statements may be written on index cards and filed so
other readers can consult them when choosing books.

Response Journals

To emphasize the personal experience of a book, especially the aesthetics of the experience, children are encouraged to keep response journals. There is no one way to keep a response journal. However, to prime responses, teachers can suggest that readers note parts that interested, frightened, surprised, troubled, or pleased them, or answer questions like these:

What feelings did you experience during reading?
Did the story leave you feeling satisfied? Why or why not?
If you could speak to the author of the book, what would you say or ask?
Were events in the story similar to occurrences in your own life?
Have you read, heard, or seen a story like this one?
Would you read another book by this author?

Some students will want to note in their journals words or phrases that caught their attention. Young children may respond with pictures and dictated statements before they have facility with writing. They should also be encouraged to write as much as they can on their own; this is a place where invented spelling is entirely acceptable. The response journal is like a diary, to be shared with the owner's permission and never to be graded.

The Teacher's Record Keeping

The teacher keeps anecdotal records of conferences; these become the basis for small-group and individual directed reading and skill-building lessons. Such general things as enthusiasm, interest, and articulateness are noted. If the child reads aloud, the process provides valuable clues about reading strengths and weaknesses, as follows:

Does the child show anxiety or discomfort during the reading?
Does the child read with appropriate expression, making use of punctuation, thus indicating that what is being read is understood?
Is the reading word-by-word or in meaningful word groupings?

If the child makes miscues (substitutions, omissions, etc.),
   do they change the sense of what is being read?
Does the child notice and attempt to correct miscues?

Some teachers find it useful to periodically tape record samples of children's oral reading so children (and parents) can chart
progress throughout the year. Tape recordings are also useful in
self-evaluation.

Creative and Literary Responses

Although reading a book for pleasure can be its own reward,
after some books children enjoy responding to art with art: writing,
drawing, dramatizing, sculpting, creating (or at least planning
through storyboards) videotapes or films, making games. The following is a sampling of the dozens of possible responses:

- Writing reviews like those found in magazines and newspapers (a real-life activity unlike the book report, which is
  found only in classrooms)
- Writing a sequel to a story
- Creating a Readers Theater script by extracting dialogue
  from a particularly funny or interesting scene, xeroxing it,
  cutting it in strips and arranging it on a sheet in the form
  of a playlet, with narration where necessary
- Making oaktag mobiles with pictures illustrating key scenes
  from the story
- Writing and illustrating an advertisement for the book
- Writing a fan letter to the author
- Planning a TV mini-series based on a book: choosing the
  scenes, casting the characters, designing the set
- Creating a family tree for the characters in the book
- Drawing and lettering a pictorial map that shows the story's
  setting
- Making paper cutouts and clothing for the main charac-
  ters in the book.
- Creating a sequence game for others to play by sketching
  key scenes on file cards for players to lay out in order
- Writing a poem about the story or a character in the story

In this chapter we have considered the experience of literature and initial responses to it. Criticism is centered in knowledge.

One's sense of story grows with experience of story. Developing a sense of story through listening, reading independently, and responding through talk and art is central to criticism. But wide reading without study leaves readers in the same position as that of pianists who play by ear. They know when it sounds right, but critics grow through study. What this constitutes is the subject of the next chapter.

8

Growing as Critics

The critic's function is to interpret every work of literature in the light of all the literature he knows, to keep constantly struggling to understand what literature as a whole is about.

—Northrop Frye (1963a, p. 44)

To understand what literature as a whole is about students need to engage in a process of discovering for themselves how literature is unified. In Chapters 6 and 7 we explored what I consider to be the first phase of criticism: broad experience of imaginative literary works. Experience elicits response, which is also an aspect of criticism. First experiences and responses are or ought to be centered on the aesthetics of the works of art and their affect. The next phase of criticism involves an exploration of the unifying principles of literature, as delineated in Part II of the book. This chapter suggests how—with no diminution of the aesthetic experience—this exploration may be accomplished.

LEARNING THROUGH DISCUSSION

Talking is a major way in which students express their responses to literature and—through the process—amplify, clarify, and extend those responses, while at the same time working their way into a deeper understanding both of a particular work and of general literary principles. Time for purposeful talk after the experience of literature is analogous to the lab after a presentation in science. It is a time for experimenting with ideas, exploring concepts, making observations, and drawing conclusions.

Generally, an oral rather than a written response to the literature read or listened to is preferable for elementary and middle
school students. Young children for whom extensive writing can
be physically taxing are likely to regard lengthy written answers
to reams of questions, character studies, and plot summaries as
punishment.

Literary study involves *exploration* of ideas, *sharing* of responses, and *growth through reflection*. Through purposeful group
discussions, these characteristics of literary study—literary criticism—are better realized and developed. One important aspect
of literary study is expressing ideas—orally and in writing—about
stories, poems, and other literary works. A major goal of the study
is to develop the ability to articulate the ideas and feelings literature elicits.

The process of discussion must be taught; children cannot
be expected to come to class with mastery of this difficult but profitable technique. Discussion has two major emphases: courtesy
and participation. Children need to practice the ritual give-and-
take that discussion requires. They need to learn to listen, wait
their turns, assimilate and weigh what they have heard, and build
upon this when they speak. From their first encounter with a new
class, teachers need to work to establish a climate of mutual
respect where ideas and opinions are heard and valued. This is
particularly important in literary studies where, if the discussion
is in response to questions that require genuine reflection and
critical thinking (as they ought to be), there are no "right" and
"wrong" answers.

Talking in Small Groups

A distinction needs to be made between small- and large-
group discussion. Whole-class discussion, unless it follows discussion in small groups, is unlikely to be more than exchange
among a few. Only a limited number of students in a class of
average size can participate at once, comments are likely to be
addressed to the teacher rather than to other pupils, and un-
engaged minds are apt to wander. Children of all ages can be
taught to work together in small groups.

The group process is an invaluable one where children have
the opportunity to express their ideas, to test their notions in
relation to those of others, and to engage in divergent and convergent thinking. In the group process, ideas are amended, elabo-

rated upon, defended, and supported. Children, with guidance, learn to summarize, to synthesize, to qualify. They also benefit from exposure to others' vocabulary and usage (Cohen, 1986).

Work groups for literary or any study are best if they are heterogeneous, with their composition frequently changed. Slower learners should have the opportunity to work with faster learners in an atmosphere of mutual help and support; the least articulate and the verbally facile will mutually benefit from working together. Common interests, personal preferences, and individual needs will also determine the composition of groups. Research has determined that five is the optimal group size (Cohen, 1986).

Learning to work cooperatively in groups is a developmental process, with first experiences planned for success. With the teacher's help, the children themselves can develop the ground rules that will govern their small-group work. The first small-group activity might well be a session in which groups work on these rules, subsequently pooling their ideas in a large-group sharing session.

The Teacher's Role

Effective teachers help to create the structure of a subject in students' minds. The unifying principles of literature are the teacher's deductive framework. Aware of the principles, the teacher devises learning sequences that allow students to inductively discover them.

As an example, suppose a group of fourth graders have all read the same novel, *Stone Fox* (Gardiner, 1980). Provided with a set of questions that apply to novels in general—a selection, say, from the questions listed in Chapter 7—they meet in small groups to discuss the novel.

Teachers do need to work with the children to set specific purposes and establish time limits. In the beginning, short sessions are advisable. To be avoided is the ruin of the process when bored participants, talked out, turn to paper planes, spitballs, or harassment of others.

Once a clear purpose has been established for a group-talk session, teachers function as facilitators of discussion. Circulating from group to group, they sit in for a time to facilitate the group process and provide information as requested by the children. Offering quantities of unsolicited information is to be avoided.

In facilitating the group process the teacher may

- Encourage participation: "Has everyone given an opinion on that point?" "Mary, do you agree with what's been said so far?"
- Ask for qualification: "Your idea about the character is interesting, Mario. What was your reason for thinking that?"
- Help the children to get at the thinking behind comments, by asking "Why?" and encouraging group members to do the same of each other.
- Handle the monopolizer with a tactful but firm comment: "Wait a minute, Kyle; Sheena isn't finished."
- Encourage group members or the designated leader to summarize ideas.

More structured discussion may be an outgrowth of children's free responses. Teachers need to listen closely to questions and comments children make after they hear a story or poem. These will be fruitful starting points for small-group discussion conducted independently or led by the teacher. Sometimes these comments lead to purely literary discussions: "That ending just doesn't follow from what went before." At other times, comments may signal the need for research and further talk: "How long do elephants usually live?"

LEARNING SEQUENCES IN LITERARY CRITICISM: DISCUSSION

A learning sequence may be a single session or series of sessions, depending on its purpose. It may be a discussion or another type of activity, such as those suggested later in this chapter. Sometimes teachers will serve only as facilitators in group discussions, as outlined above. At other times, a more structured discussion may be required; these are led by the teacher.

In the latter case, to help students toward an understanding of literary principles, teachers may select poems and stories for presentation that exemplify the principle the teachers want the children to inductively grasp. Through careful questioning, teachers lead the discussion as suggested in the following examples.

Conventional Patterns in Story

The aim of the session is to lead young children toward an understanding that stories come in conventional "shapes."

Teacher: We have read *Where the Wild Things Are* (Sendak, 1963) and *The Tale of Peter Rabbit* (Potter, 1902). It's true that they are stories about very different things, but let's think about ways in which they are alike.
Children:
- Max and Peter have adventures.
- They get into danger.
- Lots of things happen to them.
- They get home okay in the end.
- Everything ends happy, except Peter is sent to bed.
- But he did okay; he got away from Mr. McGregor.
- Max didn't really go away; he had a dream.
- But he went away in his dream; it's the same thing.

Teacher: If you were to draw the shape of the two stories, what shape would it be?
Children:
- They both end up where they started.
- Max leaves his room but he comes back to it.
- So does Peter.
- They both leave home, have adventures, and come back.
- Then it's a circle; the stories are shaped like a circle.

Teacher: Do you know any other stories with that shape?
Children:
- In "Jack and the Beanstalk," Jack goes to the giant's castle and comes back home.
- In *Sylvester and the Magic Pebble* [Steig, 1969], Sylvester in the end gets to be himself again, home with his parents.
- Even E.T. gets to go home at the end of the movie!

The Quest as a Shaper of Stories

The aim in the following discussion is to help older students discover how the hero story relates to the dialectical aspect of literary structure. The quest of heroes and heroines involves efforts to restore harmony, right a wrong, or find their own sense of identity.

Teacher: The old tale we just read, about Gilgamesh, the Sumerian king who searched for everlasting life, is a typical hero story. Think of other hero stories you know. How are they alike?

Students:

• The hero goes searching for something important to him, like Sir Lancelot looking for the Holy Grail.
• Or Jason searching for the Golden Fleece.
• Sometimes he tries to get rid of a monster.
• The way Perseus does when he goes after Medusa.
• Or St. George when he kills the dragon.
• Sometimes the hero isn't happy with the way things are, so he sets out to change them.
• Moses did that.
• So did Robin Hood.
• The heroes in fairytales go to seek their fortune.
• In *Arrow to the Sun* [McDermott, 1978], the boy has to find his father to prove his identity.
• Heroes and heroines are always looking to change things.
• To make things better.
• A hero story has some kind of search in it.
• Or a test. The hero has to prove his courage.
• Sometimes there's a search *and* a test; Hercules has to survive 12 tests if he wants to keep on living.

Teacher: Your examples are all from ancient hero tales. Is it the same for modern stories?

Students:

• Superman sets out to right wrongs.
• So does Luke Skywalker.
• In *Dicey's Song* [Voight, 1982], Dicey takes her family on a long journey to their grandmother's when her mother disappears.
• In *Call It Courage* [Sperry, 1940], Mafatu thinks he's a failure, so he leaves home, maybe to die, but he finds out that he has courage.
• In *Dogsong* [Paulsen, 1985], Russel and his dog team escape modern life to find their own true song.

Conventional Characters

Through examination of the hero story, the concept of recurrent character types may be developed. As discussed in Chapter 4, the evil goddess of the myth is related to the witch of the romance, to the evil stepmother of fairytales, and to the impossible female parent of modern realistic stories in the ironic mode. The helpful goddess of myth, the kindly sorceress of romance, the fairy godmother of the fairytale, and the kindly mother figure in the modern realistic story are also related.

Children will discover that certain types of characters are associated positively with the hero or heroine's quest, while some are aligned against it. Some characters exist to make main characters look more heroic, to give them help, even to give them someone to talk to. Children will note that there may be neutral, flat, or static characters in many stories who play a small role in moving the story forward.

The aim in the following discussion is to help younger students discover that certain character types are important to the structure of stories.

Teacher: What gets most stories going?
Students:
- You have to have some kind of problem to get it started.
- Sometimes there's a war, kind of, between two kinds of people: good guys and bad guys.
- A story usually has good guys and bad guys.
- Or good girls and bad girls.
- A lot of stories are just struggles between people on one side and people on the other.

Teacher: We just read one of Dr. Seuss' first books, *The 500 Hats of Bartholomew Cubbins* [Seuss, 1938]. Is there a "bad guy" in that story?
Student: The Grand Duke Wilfred.
Teacher: Why is he in the story?
Students:
- He makes it interesting because he's so cruel and nasty.
- Mean characters are usually interesting, even though you don't like them much.
- Like Templeton the rat in *Charlotte's Web* [White, 1952].
- Wilfred in this story is the opposite to Bartholomew; he's a bully and Bartholomew is basically just an innocent nice guy.
- He's the opposite too because he's rich and royal and Bartholomew is poor and ordinary.
- That makes you wonder how things will turn out. Wilfred has all the power.

- He puts suspense into the story because he threatens Bartholomew's life.
- You need somebody like him in a story because it's someone for the main character to fight against.
- You need that for a good story.

Charles Bullock (personal communication, 1986), who teaches Navajo and Zuni children in New Mexico, reports a discussion with his upper-elementary students.

> We just finished Scott O'Dell's *Sing Down the Moon* [1970]. Toward the end, Polly asked, "What happened to Nehana?" We all then realized that she had just disappeared from the story. Several students offered ideas of what became of her. The students discovered on their own that some characters play small but important parts, entering a story just long enough to help move the story in a certain direction (Sloan, 1984, 105).

Ann, a middle school teacher (personal communication, 1989), reports a learning sequence—based on suggestions in an earlier edition of *The Child as Critic*—on the trickster character in literature. To get her aliterate seventh graders to read, she asked them to find in picture books examples of the character of the trickster in traditional literature. By way of introduction, she read to them several Afro-American folktales featuring the archetypal trickster, Brer Rabbit. Student examples included Puss in Boots, Anansi, and Molly Whuppie. Discussion of this ubiquitous character took place in a learning sequence that lasted several weeks, with high student involvement.

The students discovered that there were good and evil tricksters; they were able to describe the traits of the character type. They enjoyed identifying reincarnations of the character in contemporary stories: Gilly in *The Great Gilly Hopkins* (Paterson, 1978) and Charlotte in *Charlotte's Web* (White, 1952). As a culmination, the class prepared a genealogy chart on the trickster, including on it examples of the character taken from traditional and contemporary literature, television shows, films, and cartoons.

Patterns of Imagery

As discussed in Chapter 4, two structures underlie literary imagery. The cyclical pattern is exemplified in the association of

certain seasons and times of year with particular stories or parts
of stories. Beginnings and quests, for instance, are likely to take
place in the "merry months" of May and June, as in the old ballads. Endings and failures are often associated with the "death"
of the year: fall and winter. Triumph, the full powers of the hero,
and the like are most often associated with "high summer," when
nature is also at her peak of growth and beauty.

A dialectical structure is also present in literary imagery.
People's dreams and desires are associated with gardens and
visions of paradise; their nightmares with deserts, threatening forests, and wastelands. Settings reflect atmosphere and mood.

Some colors are associated with dreams; others with nightmares. Dark colors may have sinister associations because the
darkness of night can cause fear; the golden light of the sun is
reassuring. Peaceful animals and birds like the lamb and the dove
are on the side of good in stories; serpents and ravens typically
belong with the evil side.

Three examples of learning sequences dealing with imagery
follow.

Sequence for Primary Grades.   The aim of the first sequence
is to help young children develop some awareness of patterns of
imagery in stories.

Teacher: Let's try a game, something like "Twenty Questions," on
the stories we know. The categories are animal, vegetable,
and mineral. Which animals are "good" characters in stories?
Which aren't?

Students:
- Animals that are used to being with people, like the horse
  in "The Goose Girl."
- Or the cat in "Puss in Boots."
- Pigs are good! There's Padre Porko.
- And Charlotte the spider.
- Foxes are pretty bad. One ate the Gingerbread Boy.
- Wolves are bad, in stories anyway. One eats Red Riding
  Hood's grandmother.
- Dogs are always good.

Teacher: Think about the natural surroundings in stories you
know, the trees and plants and the ground around them.
What are they like in the stories you know?

Students:
  • When Dominic [Steig, 1972] was in danger, he was deep in a forest.
  • So was Red Riding Hood.
  • Rapunzel was sent away to a forest and then to a kind of desert where nothing grew.
  • No sun ever shone on the place where Medusa lived.
  • Sylvester turned into a rock, the opposite of being alive.
  • And he felt loneliest in the winter when the ground was cold and covered with snow.
  • But snow can be part of a happy story, like *The Snowy Day* [Keats, 1962]. It depends.
  • And forests are okay if your home is in the forest.
  • A lot of stories end up with people in castles.
  • Or at home where they're comfortable.

Sequences for Upper Elementary and Middle School Grades.
The aim of the next sequence is to help students toward an understanding of the dialectic structure underlying literary works.

Teacher: Stories show the difference between our dreams—what we want most—and our nightmares—what we fear and dread. In your experience, is that a true statement? Let me hear your thoughts on it.
Students:
  • Stories usually begin with a problem or a situation where things aren't all they should be.
  • People want to change that.
  • Take slavery. Books about Harriet Tubman, like *Freedom Train* [Sterling, 1954], show how she leads people out of a nightmare to safety.
  • *The Girl in the Box* [Sebestyen, 1988] leaves you feeling depressed because what happens to her is a nightmare that doesn't have an end.
  • The same thing with *The Year Without Michael* [Pfeffer, 1987]. He's still missing at the end of the book.
  • But most stories move from bad to good, from what isn't wanted by the main characters to what is wanted.
  • A lot of times it's all too easy. Things work out well as if by magic. That's not true to life.
  • And some stories show only the nightmare side and that

leaves you feeling down. *The Bumblebee Flies Anyway* [Cormier, 1983] is like that.
  • Even in that story there's a dream of what could be and the boy tries to make the dream happen.

The aim of the following sequence is to help middle school age students discover in literary works patterns of imagery that reflect natural cycles.

Teacher: In nature, what happens in spring and summer?
Students:
  • Plants grow. Leaves come out.
  • Everything is alive.
  • Things are green and growing.
Teacher: What happens in fall and winter to natural things like plants?
Students:
  • Leaves die and fall.
  • Nothing grows.
  • The sky is often grey.
  • The wind is cold.
Teacher: Think about this: Even though they may not mention the seasons directly, stories might be described as being spring/summer or fall/winter stories. Or, to put it another way, during the course of a story, the action may move from spring/summer to fall/winter and perhaps back again to spring.
Students:
  • "The Ugly Duckling" is a good example of the way a story moves from winter to spring. It's springtime when the happy ending comes.
  • *Beauty and the Beast* is the same.
  • At the beginning of "The Sleeping Beauty," everyone is asleep, almost as though they were dead. When the Prince comes and kisses the Princess, everyone wakes up and the thorn hedge around the castle starts to bloom.
  • A lot of stories move in circles like the seasons. For awhile everything looks dead, the way it does in fall and winter, but at the end, things are brighter.
  • Some stories never get brighter, like *Slake's Limbo* [Holman, 1974]. At the end the boy is still a homeless person.
  • But there's some hope, because at least he has moved out of the depths of the subway.

- In some stories, the main character dies or almost dies, but reappears at the end.
- In the myth about the god, Osiris [McDermott, 1977], he dies, but he is actually brought back to life again.
- In *Call It Courage* [Sperry, 1942], life is pretty cold and harsh for Mafatu in the beginning. He even wants to die. But at the end, he comes home a new person.
- You could say he was reborn.

Associative Language

The literary imagination seeks to associate and identify the human mind with what goes on outside it. The language of literature is associative, using simile and metaphor to express this identity. In the imaginative logic of literary thought and language, therefore, two unlike things may be said to be like each other or to be each other. (My love is like a rose; my love is a rose.)

The logic of metaphor, which insists that "this is that," is not the logic of reason; it is an *imaginative* logic that illustrates how the imaginative writer goes beyond nature to show a world absorbed and possessed by the human mind. In poetry, for instance, it is not only legitimate but highly desirable to tell the "truth" by means of analogy and association—truth that cannot be defended or refuted in discursive terms. Poetic expression, which uses associative language to make its own sense, should be regarded by children as a valid mode of expression, and not as a distortion of prose. If children are able to grasp this basic understanding of poetic expression in elementary and middle school, problems of understanding or accepting the "difficult" images of the poets in high school and beyond may be minimized.

Children ought to become aware of the logic of metaphorical language in literature, not by collecting similes and metaphors as if they were so many colorful pebbles, but by seeing for themselves, as they read and write, the worth and value of using concrete and sensory imagery to express ideas.

Sequence for Primary Grades. In the following discussion, the teacher leads young children toward an awareness that the literary imagination seeks to suggest an identity between the human mind and the world outside it by using metaphor, the language of identification: this is that.

Teacher: Just before class I saw Peter galloping across the school-
yard. You looked happy.

Student: I was pretending to be a horse, a really fast one like I saw
on Saturday at the race track. Running makes me feel good.

Teacher: Yes. Now I want everyone to act out for us what feeling
happy is like for you. Let's push back the chairs and tables
to have room to move. Now, show us with your whole body
what feeling happy is like. (The teacher might provide music as the children proceed with movement mimes, some in
place, others moving about the room.)

Teacher: I saw lots of happy, freed-up people just now. Mary, were
you flying?

Students:
- I was. I was a bird.
- I was floating like a cloud.
- I was a fish swimming.
- I was a rabbit running.
- I was sunshine.
- I was a tree getting blown by the wind.
- I was swinging in a swing.
- I was singing a song.

Teacher: Everybody acted out feeling free and happy by being
something else. I wonder why.

Students:
- That's the way you have to do it.
- If I just stand here feeling happy you couldn't tell. I had to
  pretend I was a leaf twirling around in the air.

Teacher: In order to show what it's like to be happy, you have to
use a comparison. That is, you say that feeling happy is like
other things or is other things. Let's put into words what you
acted out. (Teacher prints "Happiness is . . ." on an experience chart or the board and records the children's responses
under these words.)

Students:
- Happiness is flying like a bird.
- Happiness is a leaf twirling in the wind.
- Feeling happy is the warm sun.
- A balloon!
- The sound of the bell on the ice-cream truck.
- A ride on a swing.
- Happy is the smell of roast turkey cooking.
- Happy is eating ice cream.

Teacher: Do you know what? We've made a poem by saying what happy is like. You did just what poets do. Who can explain what I mean?

Students:
- We said that feeling happy was like something.
- We said feeling happy was something else.
- We said feeling happy was smelling or tasting something.
- Or something you can hear.
- Or even taste.

Teacher: Let's read our poem.

Sequence for Upper Elementary and Middle School Grades. The aim of the discussion is to lead the students to an understanding that certain patterns of imagery are associated with the expression of positive and negative feelings. The students have experienced a number of poems of their own and of the teacher's choosing, including the following:

HERE WE COME A-PIPING

Here we come a-piping,
In Springtime and in May;
Green fruit a-ripening,
And Winter fled away.
The Queen she sits upon the strand,
Fair as a lily, white as a wand;
Seven billows on the sea,
Horses riding fast and free,
And bells beyond the sand.

Traditional

CITY AUTUMN

The air breathes frost. A thin wind beats
Old dust and papers down gray streets
And blows brown leaves with curled-up edges
At frightened sparrows on window ledges.
A snow-flake falls like an errant feather:
A vagabond draws his cloak together,
And an old man totters past with a cane
Wondering if he'll see Spring again.

Joseph Moncure March

DARK GIRL

Easy on your drums,
Easy wind and rain,
And softer on your horns,
She will not dance again.

Come easy little leaves
Without a ghost of sound
From the China trees
To the fallow ground.

Easy, easy drums
And sweet leaves overhead,
Easy wind and rain;
Your dancing girl is dead.

Arna Bontemps

IN TIME OF SILVER RAIN

In time of silver rain
The earth
Puts forth new life again,
Green grasses grow
And flowers lift their heads,
And over all the plain
The wonder spreads
        Of life,
        Of life,
        Of Life!

In time of silver rain
The butterflies
Lift silken wings
To catch a rainbow cry,
And trees put forth
New leaves to sing
In joy beneath the sky
As down the roadway
Passing boys and girls
Go singing, too,

In time of silver rain
> When spring
> And life
> Are new.

Langston Hughes

LAUGHING SONG

When the green woods laugh with the voice of joy,
And the dimpling stream runs laughing by;
When the air does laugh with our merry wit,
And the green hill laughs with the noise of it;

When the meadows laugh with lively green,
And the grasshopper laughs in the merry scene,
When Mary and Susan and Emily
With their sweet round mouths sing "Ha, Ha, He!"

When the painted birds laugh in the shade,
Where our table with cherries and nuts is spread,
Come live and be merry and join with me,
To sing the sweet chorus of "Ha, Ha, He!"

William Blake

Teacher: Think of the poems we have shared lately. What were some of the subjects they dealt with?

Students:
- They talked about people.
- And animals.
- A lot of them were nature poems.
- I think most of them expressed feelings.

Teacher: What feelings do they express?

Students:
- Sadness, sometimes, like in the poem "Dark Girl." It's gloomy, because, after all, she's dead.
- So is "City Autumn" sad. It makes you think of dark, rainy days. There's not much hope in it.
- Some of the poems we heard were happy, though.
- Yeah. Like "Laughing Song" and the one by Langston Hughes, "In Time of Silver Rain."
- Most of the poems we read by e. e. cummings were happy, like the one that starts, "In just-spring."

Teacher: In the poems we read and others you know, what sea-
   son is associated with positive feelings? negative feelings?
Students:
   • Spring! That's in Blake's "Laughing Song."
   • And in "Here We Come A-Piping."
   • The sadder poems usually mention fall when the leaves are
     falling and things are dying. Like "City Autumn."
   • Or it's the coldest time of the year the way it is in "The
     Ballad of the Harp-Weaver" [Millay, 1924].
Teacher: Why would this be so?
Students:
   • In spring and summer grass and trees are alive and grow-
     ing. In a poem about death, you'd probably not want to
     describe a season like that.
   • You'd want images from fall and winter when nature sleeps
     or dies.
   • Images of cold wind and frozen ground go better with sor-
     row than images of sunshine and spring rain.
   • Unless you want a contrast.
Teacher: Can you say more about that idea?
Students:
   • Let's say you were writing a poem about a baby's death. If
     you said it took place on a beautiful, sunny day, it seems
     to me it would make the death even harder to take.
   • I agree. There's a contrast like that in "The Ballad of the
     Harp-Weaver." The boy's mother dies on Christmas Eve,
     which is supposed to be a happy time.
   • It's also the coldest time in many parts of the world:
     midwinter.
   • Right. The poem makes the point that it's the worst winter
     for cold in history.
Teacher: I like your ideas.

Making Connections

   Charles Bullock (personal communication, 1986) encourages
his students to make connections among the books they read and
hear. At the time of Martin Luther King, Jr.'s birthday, he read
aloud to the children three biographies about the civil rights
leader. The children enjoyed comparing the authors' differing
styles in telling basically the same story. Some time after the reading, this discussion took place.

Teacher: What do you remember about Martin Luther King, Jr.?
Students:
- When he was small, he wanted to learn big words.
- He told his mom, "I'm going to get me a lot of big words."
- When he fought, he didn't use guns or bombs. He just used his words.
- Charlotte, in *Charlotte's Web* (White, 1952), was kind of like Martin Luther King,

Teacher: How were they alike?
Students:
- When she was trying to save Wilbur's life, she put words in her spider web. People thought it was a miracle.
- Yeah. She used big words like Martin Luther King.

Sometime later the class asked that *Wanted Dead or Alive: The Story of Harriet Tubman* (McGovern, 1977) be read aloud, on the recommendation of Shawna, who had read the book on her own. The chapter on the Civil War concluded with the words, "Now all men were free at last."

Jeremy said, "Free at last. Free at last. Thank God Almighty, I'm free at last."

The children nodded, recalling the oft-discussed lines from Martin Luther King, Jr.'s tomb. Before lunch, the teacher offered to read a poem. Shawna picked at random "Stopping by Woods on a Snowy Evening" by Robert Frost (1978). As they recalled the words on Martin Luther King, Jr.'s tomb, the last stanza had special significance for the class.

> The woods are lovely, dark and deep,
> But I have promises to keep.
> And miles to go before I sleep.
> And miles to go before I sleep.

After listening to the lines, April commented, "That poem sounds like it was written about Harriet Tubman helping the slaves escape." On request, the lines were read two more times; the other children agreed with April.

Encouraging students to make connections among the literary works they know is essential to their growth as critics. As they note these relationships, they begin to develop an awareness of the unity of all literature.

LEARNING SEQUENCES IN LITERARY CRITICISM: ACTIVITIES

The following are activities designed to develop an understanding of the unifying principles of literature, as delineated in Part II. Although they may involve discussion, they go beyond it into other areas of response.

Classification and Categorization

It will help students to become aware of recurrent archetypal structures, patterns, and themes if they work to classify in various ways what they read and hear.

• Working in groups, students might classify characters according to their power of action: Is it greater than a human's, less, about the same? Comic and cartoon characters should be included: Superman is like a god, Charlie Brown is an ordinary chap.

• Another profitable critical activity involves collecting examples of literary archetypes from television, comics, advertising, and films. As examples: the detergent that fights dirt as the knight fought the dragon; images of paradise in soft-drink commercials; cars that are cougars and rabbits; hand cream that magically transforms chapped hands; the "Cinderella" story: a young man can't get a date until the "fairy godmother" in the form of the right mouthwash transforms him.

• Students can identify archetypal plots such as the "Cinderella" story or the "Jack-the-Giant-Killer" story in television serials or soap operas, movies, comic strips, and advertisements. Examples: The "Cinderella" plot is found in many advertisements for cosmetics, which show magical transformations that result in the conquest of a lover; the "Jack-the-Giant-Killer" plot is in the episodes of Batman and Superman.

• Stories may be classified in a number of ways, the sophistication of the classifications varying in accordance with the ability of grades and classes within grades. Here are some examples of categories.

Stories that end happily or sadly
Stories of successful and failed quests
Stories of dreams and of nightmares

• To make students aware of color and how it is used in people's symbolic acts, students can be asked to show how colors may have positive and negative symbolic associations. Gold (yellow) is positive as the imperial color in the Far East, wealth, and light; negative as deceit, cowardice, and treason. Red is positive as courage, love, and fervor; negative as violence, revolt, and sin (scarlet letter "A"). Positively, purple is associated with royal dignity, wisdom, and religious leaders; negatively, with mourning. Green may stand positively for hope, growth, and life, but negatively for jealousy.

The students might exchange their ideas on why brides, graduates, and surrender flags use white; why sailors wear blue and Brownies wear brown; what colors are used on flags to signify danger and why; why red is used on valentines; why mourners wear black (do they do so in every culture?); what colors are associated with Halloween, Thanksgiving, Christmas, and so on, and why.

• As exercises in the study of archetypal imagery, students can create picture essays of comic or happy visions of life, or tragic or sad visions of life. (Refer to Table 4.1 in Chapter 4.) Happy visions are characterized by images of communion, friendship, love, and marriage; domesticated animals; gardens, parks, roses, lotus, and groves; temples, precious stones, and castles. Sad visions usually involve bullying villains, betrayed heroes and heroines, and isolated people; preying animals and birds; sinister forests, desolate wastelands, and littered city streets; deserts, rocks, and ruins.

Analysis

Criticism may focus on analysis of literary and nonliterary experiences. These activities are intended as oral exercises.

• Students can analyze movies, television dramas, or serials, using the following questions: Does the story show an upward or downward movement? What is the condition of the characters as the story begins? What is their state at the end? Is the imaginative view of the human situation basically happy and triumphant, or tragic and futile?

Are any of the following archetypes found in the stories: the dream that tells something about reality; the perilous journey in quest of something; someone expelled from society for a crime; the messenger who speaks from the world of the dead; the death of a noble person; the slaying of a monster; the transforming power of faith and love; betrayal of an innocent; recognition of a truth that changes someone's life; the idea that good action is rewarded, and so on.

• To introduce the dialectical principle, students can explore the metaphorical significance of the prepositions *up* and *down* in language and literature. Moses goes down into the land of Egypt; Elijah's chariot goes up; when we're sad, we're down, and when we're happy, we're up; a book by Booker T. Washington is called *Up From Slavery*; the prisoner-singer sings from "Down in the Valley"; Jacob saw a ladder going up to heaven; Rapunzel let her hair down so her love could climb up to her in the tower; Moses received the Ten Commandments on top of Mt. Sinai.

• Students might compare contemporary fiction with folk-tales to see how ancient archetypes appear in modern stories: the magical talisman; the curse or spell; the pattern of three attempts or three trials; transformations; mistaken identity or disguise; character types like the trickster, the underdog, the noodlehead; the triumph of good over evil. Some examples are

> James Bond's elaborate technological devices are magical in effect, like the magic talisman of the ancient hero—a cloak or helmet that causes invisibility, a sword that never misses its mark.
> Luke Skywalker has with him the same "Force" that has sustained heroes of all times.
> Yoda, one of the wise old men of literature, is Luke's teacher and advisor.
> In police shows there are often three tries to catch a killer.
> Situation comedies are filled with stock characters like the henpecked husband, the buffoon, the heartless female.
> In countless stories, good triumphs over evil, if only in the last few seconds of a show.

Critical Response Through Art, Drama, and Speech

Working in groups, students may make the following kinds of response to the literature they experience.

• To explore patterns of imagery, students might develop picture essays (with drawings or magazine pictures) that show positive and negative images: straight roads or mazes; trees in bloom or rows of telephone poles; domesticated animals and beasts or birds of prey; homes and prisons; productive people and derelicts; gentle waterfalls and destructive floods; human compassion and human cruelty.

• In a debate on the issue, "There are no heroes or heroines in modern life," students can consider the following questions: What is the definition of a hero or heroine? Has this definition changed over time? If there are modern heroes or heroines in real life, who are they? Who are our fictional heroes and heroines? Can anyone be a hero or heroine? How?

• Students can create "Me" collages with drawings or magazine pictures. Students find images from the animal, vegetable, and mineral worlds with which they identify: dog, whale, elephant, mouse; artichoke, tomato, turnip, cabbage; jewel, rock, razor. Crests may be made to adorn the collages, showing pictorially the meaning of a student's name. (Sally Smith uses a picture of a blacksmith on her crest.) A variation of the exercise is to divide the collage into two parts: "Me" and "Not Me." The opposing images show what the person rejects or does not identify with.

• Groups might dramatize, through mime, interesting metaphors from their reading. As in charades, the team acts out the metaphor while the others guess.

• To a drumbeat, students can mime changes (transformations). The leader says, "You are holding something very hot; as the beat slows, it changes into a small, pointed object; as the beat quickens, it becomes a bird or butterfly that is set free."

• With movement and mime, students can transform themselves imaginatively in quick succession into three different objects: a baby, a rock, a swaying tree.

THE UNIT APPROACH TO LITERARY STUDY

The unit—a sustained learning sequence—is an effective way to integrate language arts activities and to help young critics grow in making connections among literary works. The unit is built around a set of books, say three to five, related by theme, plot, structure, topic, focus, style, or any other common element. Through the use of carefully planned units, students learn that "in literature you don't just read one poem or novel after another, but enter into a complete world of which every work of literature is a part" (Frye, 1963a, p. 27).

The ways of organizing units are unlimited. The study in social studies of colonial America is enhanced by a unit that features several of the fine books in historical fiction dealing with the period. Great literary themes like survival or basic literary archetypes like the quest provide significant focus for units of study. Such diverse topics as bedtime, giants, friendship, or peer relationships are only a few of the countless choices available. A study of literary types, such as the fable or the cautionary tale, is another way of setting up a unit. To focus on several works by the same author is still another organizing principle, as is organization around a type of discourse such as biography, drama, journals, memoirs, and correspondence.

The three to five core books or works are read aloud in part or, preferably, in their entirety to the whole group. These listening and discussing sessions are an important feature of the unit approach. The books chosen for this stage of the unit must offer ideas that are worth thinking, talking, and writing about. In style they should be worthy of emulation because student writing may be modeled on them.

The sequence for presentation is planned so that one discussion leads into the next. New stories are considered in terms of those that went before so that students may readily discover significant relationships and recurring patterns. Joy Moss (1984) suggests use of the following kinds of questions to guide discussion (for more on questioning see Chapter 7):

- *Questions that set the stage for reading.* These may involve examination of the title and illustrations. They may, for example, ask the students to predict on the basis of these. Background information is supplied and discussed.

- *Questions that focus on the basic story.* These questions ask for information that is directly stated in the text or supplied through illustrations. They also deal with who? what? where? why? and story elements such as character, plot, and setting.
- *Questions that involve interpretation.* Here students make inferences, comparisons, and generalizations. They might consider a character's motivation, for example, or the theme of a work.
- *Questions about the craft of story.* Here aspects of form and structure are considered, the genre or type of writing, the techniques of writer and illustrator.
- *Question about the interconnections in literature.* Stories are compared in terms of story elements: characters, plots, settings, themes, style. Characteristics of genres may be considered.
- *Questions that relate the story world to the student's world.* Here students give subjective responses to books, which may include putting themselves into a character's place, or they may evaluate a character's ideas in terms of their own. (Do you think Ruth made a good decision? What would you do if you had found the treasure?)

Twenty-five to 60 books on the topic or related to it are made available for independent reading. When possible, related reading should involve works in as many different types of discourse as applicable—fiction, nonfiction, poetry, songs, journals, sections of newspapers—for both the shared and independent reading. Units are planned around three main objectives, as follows: learning about literature, independent reading, and writing or other responses.

Extensions of the reading-listening experience need to have roots in the actual experience. Writing, for example, might continue the exploration of themes or ideas presented in the literature or be modeled after the selections themselves. (A unit on fables leads naturally to the creation of original fables.)

Some works—and poetry always—lend themselves to oral reading. Folktales are natural choices for dramatization. Biographies may be recast as ballads. Questions raised in a work of fiction can lead to research in informational works and result in discursive writing. Reports may involve a variety of creative responses, as in a mixed-media presentation (taped recording with homemade slides or transparencies for the overhead projector; videotaped documentary with voice-over commentary).

In teaching criticism, the holistic unit approach obviously has much to recommend it. Students move from experiencing to extending experience through writing and art. Talking together is the major means by which students examine literary works. The focus is on making connections and seeing relationships. Units provide a means of shaping and focusing literary experience in productive ways.

CONCLUSIONS

Criticism comes from the Greek *kritikos,* meaning a "judge." A judge's right to be on the bench is based on knowledge of the law. A literary critic's obligation is to know as much as possible about literature, how the parts work separately and where they fit together in the whole.

Literacy is not something that occurs as the result of reading a book or two. Nor will reading every book in the library guarantee the reader an educated imagination. The development of literacy and the education of the imagination through literature are cumulative processes resulting from a systematic and progressive study of literature. And the early study of literature must take its place in a continuum of study if the cumulative benefits of a literary education are to be realized.

Becoming a literate critic begins when we experience and respond to our first stories and poems. It continues in further response that involves exploration, reflection, and making connections. "Whatever value there is in studying literature, cultural or practical, comes from the total body of our reading, the castle of words we've built, and keep adding new wings to all the time" (Frye, 1963a, p. 39).

9

The Process of Writing

The art [of writing] cannot be learned, in the strict sense of the word, but through wide reading one can at least absorb some of the essentials. I mean, incidentally, reading everything—not just fiction but poetry (especially poetry), drama, history, biography, philosophy. By paying close attention to the way words work in the hands of the masters, and by reading copiously, one may if one is lucky (and a little gifted) acquire a style of one's own. But trying to become a writer without having been a reader is like setting forth to sail across the ocean in a boat without sails.

—William Styron (Gallo, 1977, p. 10)

Forty prominent authors were asked what they would like to see the schools do to improve the writing of students (Gallo, 1977). From those who responded, among them five recipients of Pulitzer Prizes, came a clear message: Read to write.

"The urge to write is the child of the love of reading," wrote John Hersey (p. 1). From Mary Stolz: "I have never known or known of a writer who was not a reader from the first dazzling moment when the letters assembled themselves and became the WORD" (p. 8). William Styron said, "The only absolutely indispensable factor in the teaching of writing is, it seems to me, an insistence on the necessity of *reading*" (p. 10).

These are the words of Elizabeth George Speare, twice winner of the Newbery Award for her distinguished contribution to literature for young people.

How wonderful if we could present a young writer with an intriguing Lego set of words with which to fit together his

157

thoughts! On second thought, we do have such a treasure, an inexhaustible Lego set of words. We have books (p. 24).

If physically we are what we eat, then linguistically we are what we read and hear. In one study, the researcher found, not surprisingly, that the writing of children mirrored the style used in their basal readers (Eckhoff, 1983). Since the language children listen to and read is reflected in their writing, models need to be chosen with care. They have to be the best and they must be experienced in profusion. Experiencing a single short story or even a half dozen simply is not enough for would-be story writers. They must first be caught by pleasure in language as it is used in this or any other form. Then, through extensive experience followed by reflection and discussion—criticism—they are taught by the form itself.

All this takes time, as it should. Writing—like reading—is not something one masters in a year or two or even twelve. It is, or ought to be, a process of growth and development over a lifetime.

Of necessity, writing grows out of reading. What writers write comes out of their experience with written words. Children who have never heard or read limericks can't write them because they are unfamiliar with the conventions of the form. The same is true for all literary forms, each of which shapes language in its customary ways. Criticism, which involves the study of these forms, includes writing in them.

WRITING IN THE CLASSROOM

Just as we learn to read by reading, we learn to write by writing. Therefore, opportunities to write must be plentiful. Ideally, these opportunities should grow out of the actual experience of children, especially their reading experience. In *Learning About Biographies*, Myra Zarnowski (1990) describes how extensive reading of biographies by fourth and fifth graders led directly into their writing of biography. First, they learned about the subject—in one instance, Eleanor Roosevelt—by listening to the teacher read aloud and by reading for themselves. After they had listened or read, the children wrote in their journals what impressed them most in the biographical material on Eleanor Roosevelt. In groups of four to six, they brainstormed to prepare a list of events remembered from what they had read or heard read. Then they were ready to write their own biographical "snapshots," which consisted of a picture of an event in the subject's life and a description of it. The snapshots were then arranged in chronological order for display.

The snapshot approach to writing biography is one of four approaches to writing biography described in *Learning About Biographies*. Each approach is illustrative of good practice for writers in any literary form. First, the children were immersed in their subject through an unhurried, pleasurable program of reading and listening. Then they were prepared for writing by plenty of pre-writing activities: discussing the content and form of biographies, making notes in their journals of their personal responses to the material, asking questions, reading to answer them, brainstorming for ideas and impressions, ordering and organizing. They worked in small groups, sharing first drafts and deciding how revision would improve them.

Writing, like reading, is an individual act. But research shows that small support groups help writers to flourish (Atwell, 1987; Calkins, 1986; Graves, 1983). In a classroom where there is a climate of encouragement and support, children grow by reading and listening to each other's work in a workshop setting. Oral reading of one's work makes the work come alive; rough spots are revealed through reading aloud. To know that you will have a sympathetic audience for your words is to have an added purpose for writing.

Teachers need to remember that writing is developmental. Whatever a child writes is a beginning. Like any new growth, it must be tended and encouraged. To keep it growing and developing is the important thing. Shaping and pruning can come later. Marking things right or wrong is likely to stunt growth or cut it off altogether, especially in the case of imaginative writing and journal entries. We'd do well if we brought to children's attempts at writing the same tolerance we show for their first attempts to speak.

COMPOSING POETRY AND VERSE

Young people should certainly be encouraged to write, for everyone can learn to write poetry up to a point—the point of discovering how difficult it is to write it unusually well. To get past that point is no mean achievement, as it is well past the substandard

level of naive or doggerel verse which is the usual mode of ama-
teur expression. But the purpose of such encouragement is to
breed a love of poetry, not to breed poets. (Frye, 1956, p. 290)

Literature grows out of other literature, and experience with
poetry is the best way to foster its creation. One or two poems
will not do this, Children in elementary and middle school need
to hear poetry *in quantity*. They need themselves to say it aloud;
to respond to it with movement, questions, and comment; to
become so steeped in verse that they are able to discover how
poems are made. Then they need guidance and freedom to experi-
ment with their own poetic creations.

The poet Kenneth Koch (1970), acting on the assumption that
children are natural poets, went into inner-city classrooms to help
children express their "wishes, lies, and dreams." He found it
important to take children seriously as poets.

Children have a natural talent for writing poetry and anyone
who teaches them should know that. Teaching is really not the
right word for what takes place; it is more like permitting children to discover what they already have. (p. 25)

When education for literacy is begun by developing and
releasing "something they already have," children are likely to
respond with the energy, enthusiasm, and creativity that Koch
describes in his book.

Freedom Through Form

Writing according to a form or convention is both a discipline and a freedom. Young poets' creativity is helped, not hin-
dered, by introducing them to poetic patterns and structures.

A good way to become familiar with the wide range of excellent children's poetry available today is a series of browsing sessions in the library. Many teachers find it useful to have an
anthology of personal favorites, and suggestions for compiling it
are provided in Chapter 6.

Familiarity with poetry will reveal that there are many recurrent poetic forms. The following list is only a selection of them:
rhythmic lists (rhymed and unrhymed), chants, cinquain, riddles,
concrete poems that take on the shape of what they describe,

couplets, elegies, epics, epigrams, epistles, epigraphs, found poems
(children's notes, bits of newspaper copy, scraps of conversation),
free verse (no regular beat and no rhyme), light verse, haiku,
limerick, a statement or line arranged on a page as poetry, and
exotic forms like the pantoum, rap poems, sonnets, and wordplay (Heard, 1989; Padgett, 1987).

Wide experience with any of these forms may lead to writing
in them. Examples of some of the forms follow, presented as suggested material for learning sequences, some of which will cul-
minate in writing by students.

Riddles.   Not only are the puns and wordplay of riddles
aligned to the mental processes of children, but they are also
helpful in showing children how the literary devices we call simile
and metaphor work. The French poet Mallarme's prescription for
writing poetry was to describe not the thing but the effect it produces. This is what happens in riddling.

Experience with the form can lead naturally into the creation
of original riddles. Groups may work together with a secret object
like an apple seed, a paper clip, a birthday candle, an acorn, or a
book mark. They may describe their object literally or imaginatively in terms of the effect it produces.

One group, working with an apple seed, cooperatively developed this riddle:

> From my growth came Eve's downfall;
> And from it will come health
> Without doctors.

Rhythmic Repetitions.   The child's natural propensity for
rhythmic patterns should be indulged. In response to Byrd
Baylor's *Everybody Needs a Rock* (1974), children found a personal
rock and described it as in this example:

> My rock is rough
> As rough as sandpaper;
> My rock is silent
> Like a tree;
> My rock has lines,
> Black and white,
> Like a zebra;

My rock is just right,
Palm-size.

The sonorous repetitive rhythms of the Bible supply powerful patterns to examine and try to emulate.

PSALM 150

Praise ye the Lord.
Praise God in his sanctuary:
Praise him in the firmament of his power.
Praise him for his mighty acts:
Praise him according to his excellent greatness.
Praise him with the sound of the trumpet:
Praise him with the psaltery and harp.
Praise him with the timbrel and dance:
Praise him with stringed instruments and organs.
Praise him upon the loud cymbals:
Praise him upon the high sounding cymbals.
Let everything that has breath praise the Lord.
Praise ye the Lord.

The biblical litany uses parallel arrangements of words, variation in line length supplying a rhythmic sweep when the whole
is read aloud. A holiday or holy day can be the inspiration for such
a poem, the teacher offering the starting phrase as a primer, "Let
us be thankful for . . ."

Catalogues and Lists.   Catalogue verse is as old as Homer.
Vivid imagery, the basic stuff of poetry, is the heart of it. An entire
class may participate, the younger children dictating their ideas
on a common subject while the teacher transcribes, arranging the
lines in different lengths for maximum rhythmic appeal. Children
brainstorm, trying to use as many sensory expressions as possible.
The theme might be the classroom itself; the "poem" grows with
items like "the whirr of the pencil sharpener," "the woolly smell
of damp coats drying on a winter afternoon," "songs off-key," "the
dusty taste of a chewed pencil."
    In the title poem of *Honey, I Love,* Eloise Greenfield (1978)
gives a list, in joyous rhyme, of things well-loved. Rupert Brooke's
"The Great Lover (1915)" was a stimulus for these lines:

These I have loved:
Sunlight on a cat's silken back,
Clear June days,
White sails like birds in flight across the bay,
Green trees flecked with bits of blossom,
And the icy touch of water as I dive.

Haiku. The haiku, which originated in Japan long ago, is a miniature lyric, the essence of a moment expressed in words. It is generally believed that the haiku must have 17 syllables arranged 5, 7, 5 in 3 lines. However, traditional Japanese writers of haiku count sounds, not syllables. What is important is the vivid, precise expression of an idea, in which the reader has something to look at, hear, smell, taste, or touch. Most haiku do not use metaphor.

The firefly's little light,
Circling in the warm darkness,
Makes me smile.

Cinquain. The word, from French, means "a grouping of five." The form has 5 lines with 2, 4, 6, 8, and 2 syllables, respectively. There are variations on the form, but often the first line states the subject or title, line 2 describes it, line 3 expresses an action related to it, line 4 expresses a feeling caused by it, and line 5 expresses the title in another way. A rhyming cinquain can create a humorous effect.

First snow
Surprise in fall;
Melts soon on my warm palm,
A promise of winter white days
Swirls down.

Limericks. Nonsense verse is a particular delight for children and may be used to reintroduce the joys of verse to older children who are skeptical of poetry or disenchanted through negative experiences with it. Children enjoy the bounce and speed of a limerick, recognizing with smiles its suitability for humorous subjects, and easily following its rhythmic pattern by tapping it out. They enjoy trying to fit words into the pattern of the limerick. There are many excellent examples to guide them, none better than the playful works of Edward Lear.

There was an old person of Ware,
Who rode on the back of a bear:
When they asked, "Does it trot?" he said
"Certainly not!
He's a Moppsikon, Floppsikon bear!"

Couplets, Tercets and Quatrains.   Rhyme is an aspect of poetry that need not be stressed with children. The creation of telling, vivid, fresh images is a more poetic endeavor. But children are intrigued by rhyme, and many of the poems written for them rhyme. Reading and writing rhymed couplets is an enjoyable exercise. Children will enjoy supplying the rhyming word when couplets are read aloud.

The world is so full of a number of things
I'm sure we should all be as happy as———.

Tercets are 3-line units that may rhyme in 2 lines or all 3.

Dogs are very persuasive pets:
Mine begs and flatters;
What he wants, he gets.

Quatrains are 4-line stanzas with a possibility of a variety of rhyme schemes: aabb, abab, abcb.
The class or a group within it may choose a common subject for their couplets, tercets, or quatrains, pooling their creations to make one long poem. Common topics may be descriptions of classmates, each person's impression of a common experience, or an individual expression of a dream or wish.

Ballads.   This old form has been used by storytellers for centuries. Traditionally, ballads are written in 4-line stanzas: lines 1 and 3 have four beats; lines 2 and 4 have three beats and usually rhyme, although other rhyme schemes are possible. Old ballads, like those that tell tales of Robin Hood, often have refrains, as in "Robin Hood Rescuing the Widow's Three Sons."

Now Robin Hood was to Nottingham gone,
With a link and a down, and a day.

> And there he met a silly old woman,
> Was weeping on the way.

A Bible story, myth, folktale, or an incident from current events or history might serve as a topic for classroom balladeers, working alone or in groups. Jan Shapiro, a middle school student, composed a ballad to retell the story of "The Princess and the Pea." Here is an excerpt from her 17-stanza ballad.

> One night the rain came down in sheets
> The thunder crashed and roared;
> When all at once a knock was heard,
> On Daddy's castle door.
>
> "Oh, please, kind sir," a young girl cried,
> "The night is cold and wet,
> My travelling friends have left me now,
> Misfortune I have met."
>
> The king, he let the young girl in,
> A princess, she did claim;
> She said she came from far away,
> Princess Rose Ann was her name.

Epics.   In a middle school classroom, where students worked in groups writing, critiquing, and revising their creations, many weeks were devoted to reading aloud the *Iliad* in Richmond Lattimore's translation. One 11-year-old, inspired by the historical novels of Rosemary Sutcliff, created an original epic about Marius, a young galley slave. An excerpt from "For Marius Was Free," a 75-line poem arranged in three "books," illustrates how the rhythm and poetic devices of the *Iliad* were absorbed by the poet.

> As he entered the hold, they sprang upon him,
> As lions spring upon the unwary buck,
> And they grappled with him and bound him.
> When morning dawned the boy awoke
> To feel sharp pain in his head
> Where they had struck him with a wooden club;
> Where bonds had been, there was now a shackle,

And he was chained to a bench with others, unlucky,
A slave in the galleys of
King Solomon's Navy.

As the days became weeks,
And the weeks months,
He learned the ways of the rowers
From the man Jason, who was his friend.
So also he learned to eat the black bread;
And, as the jackals fight for the scraps
On the bony carcass that is left to them
By the lions, so he fought
For the scraps left to them by his master.
But, above all, he learned to hate.
. . .

Laurence Woodruff

"Prose" into "Poetry"

An important aspect of verse is its arrangement on the page,
as this example of "prose" into "poetry" from a second-grade student illustrates. The original story looked like this:

my dog. my dog is black with white. One black paw, the
others white my dog is noisy He barks a lot and he wags a
lot. And he eats a lot. My dog is My Best Friend. We run.
We play and we have fun.

Rearranged it looked like this:

MY DOG

My dog is
Black with white
One black paw,
The others white.
My dog is
Noisy
He barks a lot
He wags a lot
And he eats a lot
My dog is

> My Best Friend
> We run
> We play
> We have fun!

An imaginative and sympathetic treatment transforms what is in prose unnecessary repetition into an element of poetry, respects the child's natural expression, and offers the encouragement to undertake more literary endeavors, poetic and otherwise.

Poetic patterns may also be created by the alert teacher from the children's conversation. These poems, transcribed on experience charts or the board, are useful as reading material and as evidence that words may be ordered in different ways. In the example below, the teacher joins a group of first graders to talk about a trip to the zoo. Transcribed on an experience chart, the conversation might look like this:

Teacher: What did you see at the zoo?
Students:
> A lion, a lion, I saw a lion.
> Monkeys.
> I saw monkeys.
> I saw lots of monkeys.
> I saw a big baboon.
> A *big* baboon!
> At the zoo
> At the zoo I saw a hippo,
> A huge old hippo.
> At the zoo. . . .

Writing should take place in a fail-free situation, where any honest effort is welcomed. Imaginative writing ought not to be used for formal evaluations. It is an outlet for personal expression; some students will be more comfortable than others in producing these works, but all should have the opportunity to try.

Composing poetry ought to be fun, its gamelike qualities always emphasized. Working with words to form is like fitting together the parts of a puzzle. As teachers, we need to emphasize poetry as wordplay. We need to focus on the fun of writing verse. In a conversation, Eve Merriam (personal communication, 1980) complained that too many teachers put poetry on a pedestal and make of it a solemn, serious study. Poetry needs to be pulled off the pedestal so students can romp with it.

WRITING IN PROSE FORMS

The knowledge of a story form and structure, acquired inductively through experience with story, is applied by students in composing original stories. Compositions are most often in words, but they can also be in movement (drama), shapes and design (graphic art), or images recorded on film or videotape. Indeed, constructing compositions without words gives children a sense of how the imagination creates artistic wholes, and these processes complement their efforts in written composition.

Young students are likely to have a greater affinity for story than for discursive forms. It is through story that they order their experience and orient themselves to the world. In the process of studying the stories of others, they learn that these constructs involve aesthetic ordering of experience through language and form. Criticism that emphasizes literary form and structure helps young writers to see that they share with all storytellers the same problems of creative construction.

Literary Forms Stimulate Creativity

In the process of ordering experience through language, children benefit from a consideration of form. Poetic patterns have been shown to be necessary input in the process of freeing children to create their own poetry; story patterns have the same function. Providing children with patterns that give shape to their imaginings saves them hours of frustration; creativity is aided, not curtailed. All too often children are required to write stories without sufficient pre-writing activities, which include examination of models and brainstorming ideas.

From their study of story, children know how story is made (see Chapter 7). Some teachers find it useful to brainstorm a cooperative story with their students. An eighth-grade class of mine developed as a group project a contemporary realistic story. Calling upon their considerable experience with realistic fiction to develop their ideas, they decided that they needed to show a strong character using her own resources to overcome obstacles that prevented her from achieving a goal. Someone suggested a plot idea: our heroine—a talented actress—wants to attend an arts camp to study acting, but her mother, convinced that acting is an unsuitable career, refuses to pay the tuition. The young actress—the students agreed to call her Meg—was endowed with charactics, determination being foremost among them. She must try, and fail, the students decided, in several schemes to raise the tuition money. Many schemes were proposed, but it was eventually decided that these had to be limited in number (they settled on three) or the plot would lose momentum.

Meg should attend the camp, it was decided after long argument, but not in the expected way. To make the story interesting, there needed to be an unexpected—but plausible—twist in the plot. Meg had made every possible effort on her own, and now, the students decided, she could use some help. In the end, Meg's drama teacher—like the wise woman or fairy godmother of older tales—makes it possible for her to attend the camp, and with her mother's blessing. In this learning sequence, which lasted several weeks, the students struggled with many artistic problems, finding the greatest difficulty in manipulating incidents to make their story plausible and believable.

Impersonal forms provide structures into which children can project feeling un-self-consciously. Impressions and experiences may be unique, but they require a conventional form for their expression in words. Ideas of what originality is are often exaggerated; the best writers have always used the forms and conventions, and even the ideas, of those who came before them. Child writers may be encouraged to do the same. They may rewrite a story in a different form—a myth as a story poem, say, or an adventure story as a play. They might retell a traditional folk- or fairytale, sometimes with a contemporary setting. The triad form of the typical folktale might be used as a pattern for a story with a modern setting. The heroic quest is not limited to ancient tales of romance, but may feature heroes and heroines very like their youthful creators, struggling to attain some worthy goal. Tall tales, with their larger-than-life characters outdoing themselves in marvelously implausible endeavors, are ready-made templates for original tales. Young writers may create their own myths of origin (*pourquoi* tales) along the lines of the myths of the ancients or following the pattern they discover by reading or listening to Kipling's (1902/1987) *Just-so Stories*.

The archetypal patterns and motifs found in stories are the building blocks for creating new tales. There are

Repetitive patterns (three trials, three journeys)
Transformations (literal and psychological)
Clashes between good and evil, with the conventional tri-
umph of the good
Contrasting characters such as the good sister-bad sister duo
of countless folktales
Conventional rewards for good or courageous behavior
Helpful characters like loyal sidekicks or wise men and women
who provide main characters with help and advice
Tricky characters who outwit
Underdogs who come out on top
Talismans and amulets that bring good luck
Prophecies, spells, and incantations

A story may be told from different points of view. Folktales, for example, are usually third-person accounts. Rewriting the tales in first person brings a new perspective to the tale and gives students firsthand knowledge of how a literary technique operates.

Stories may be recast in different forms. The journeys of the explorers can become the subject of narrative poems. Excerpts from novels may be written as plays or television scripts. Historical events may be described in letters or diaries created by students. A class newspaper, complete with editorials, feature stories, cartoons, and classified advertisements, can make another historical period come alive.

Case Studies in Composition

The following are illustrations and examples of learning sequences in which literary forms provided the patterns for original writing.

Repetitive Patterns.   A group of first graders in St. Brigid's School, Brooklyn, New York, created a story of their own using the repetitive pattern of *Do You Want to See Something?* (Merriam, 1965). The picture book text begins, "Do you want to see a dancing flea? In the circus there's a tent. In the tent there's a ring. In the ring there's a pony . . ." and so on until ". . . there's a mouse. . . . And on that mouse there is a dancing flea."

The children and the teacher, Marie Woods, read the text together several times. Then the teacher asked if the children wanted to create a story of their own using the patterns of the one they had just read. They did.

"Do you want to see new shoes?" was their first line, because a boy in their group was wearing new shoes that day. "In the city there's a school. In the school there is a classroom. In the classroom there's a boy. And on that boy, on that boy are two new shoes." Each child chose a line to copy and illustrate on a sheet of construction paper. The teacher made a cover and stapled the pages together. Soon the first graders were reading their own story (Sloan, 1980).

In a third grade class, the children read and listened to many books that used highly predictable language patterns (Sloan, 1988). As the culmination of the learning sequence, they created their own predictable books. Here is an example of a book on shapes and colors.

This color is dark blue. (Letters printed in dark blue)
And this is a triangle. (Drawing of a triangle)
So this is a dark blue triangle. (Drawing of a triangle
   colored dark blue)

The book continued through several shapes and colors.

This color is red.
And this is a circle.
So this is a red circle.

Traditional Literature as Models. Folktales, myths, and fables have provided patterns of story form for writers of every age. Here is a fourth grader's version of a familiar tale:

Once upon a time Tom Quick came to school to show off his new red sports car to his friends. He bragged about how fast it went. Tom told everyone that his new car could beat any other car in a race.

Just then, Bill Pokey drove up in his beat-up piece of junk car. Tom and his friends started teasing him about his car. Bill got out of his car and said to Tom, "I bet my old piece of junk car could beat your sports car in a race." So they agreed to have a race around town.

The race started. Tom took off very fast and Bill's car was very slow. Tom was so far down the road that he couldn't see Bill's car anymore. As he passed by McDonalds he saw some of his friends. He stopped and said to himself, "I'll win the race, so I have time for a hamburger."

Tom was having such a good time with his friends that he lost track of time and didn't see Bill drive by. At last Tom said, "I've been here too long. I'd better go." He got into his car and drove away fast.

When Tom got to the finish line, Bill was already there. Bill laughed at Tom. "I told you I could beat you!" (Curran, 1987)

Another fourth-grade class read many myths of origin, particularly those found in the mythology of native Americans: "Why the Robin Has a Red Breast," "How the Rabbit Got His Short Tail," and others. Then they wrote original myths that explained, among other things, why the grass is green, why eyes are different colors, why dogs bark, why birds sing and frogs croak.

Short Stories as Models.   One junior high school class read and studied short stories for weeks. The students and the teacher read aloud a wide selection of stories, old and new. In small groups, working inductively, the children described short story techniques: few characters, economy of expression, early establishment of setting and situation, and the like. They then discussed possible subjects for short stories.

Those who were unable to settle on a story idea were encouraged to retell myths and Bible stories with contemporary settings and characters. One boy, for example, wrote about a man called Noah, taunted by neighbors who thought him mad to be building a boat in his backyard when the nearest body of water was a meager creek on the other side of town.

STRANGE LITTLE OLD MAN

Noah Gransby was a slow, old man who could never complete anything he began. That is why his actions the past few months had puzzled the townspeople of Lamptonville. Their concern was stimulated as they watched him limp slowly, day after day, from his tiny brick house to the almost as tiny supply store across the street. They caught brief glimpses of him lugging heavy lumber daily into his barren, undernourished back yard. No one offered to help him, and most people participated freely in the loud, continuous laughing and ridiculing of Gransby.

A few reconnoitering individuals soon discovered what he was doing. But they were more puzzled by their findings. Others refused to believe it and went to see for themselves. Soon everyone in Lamptonville knew that old Noah was building a boat. A boat? It rarely rained even in the summer here, and a few inches of snow was all the precipitation in winter. And Gransby was building a deep water vessel! The nearest body of water was Craig's Creek: ten feet wide, several inches deep, and almost a mile away on the other side of town. Poor old Gransby. The townspeople had sensed his decline. Yet, why would a madman go to the extent Gransby was going to?

The sun left Lamptonville and dark clouds crawled overhead. And then one day . . . rain . . . and for forty days . . . rain. Finally, a sparkling gem of brilliance lit the sky and a rainbow hovered at the horizon. A small white dove flittered around, and beneath it, the hull of a boat sank slowly beneath the water's surface. Noah Gransby could never complete anything he began.

Peter Gross

Writing took place in class. The all-important first paragraphs were tested on others and revised again and again. Final dog-eared drafts were polished and read aloud. Proofreading was important because the stories were published for distribution to other classes and to parents. A copy of the publication, which included a short story from each student, was placed with the library's collection of short stories for circulation (Sloan, 1972).

Plays from Narratives.   A sixth-grade class enjoyed preparing scripts for Readers Theater after examining play form. Scripts were performed for other classes in the school. What follows is an example of a Readers Theater script created from the book, *Anastasia Krupnik* (Lowry, 1979).

Anastasia Krupnik

Characters: Narrator, Anastasia, her Mother and Father.

Narrator: Anastasia Krupnik is a ten-year-old girl. Her mother is a painter. Her father is a college professor and a poet. They are together in their living room.
Anastasia: Why did you have to name me Anastasia? None of the other kids can spell it, so when they have to vote by secret ballot, nobody ever votes for me. Like when I was nominated

for class secretary, only 4 people voted for me. The other 22 voted for Mary Ellen Bailey.

Father: The reason they didn't vote for you is because the class secretary has to have good handwriting. And your hand-writing looks like hieroglyphics. That time you tried to forge an absence excuse, you got caught right away, remember? Because no parent—no adult—would be caught dead with handwriting like that.

Anastasia: No adult would be caught dead with a name like Anastasia. Why did you guys name me that?

Father: Interesting question. Choosing names is a fascinating pro-cedure. Have you chosen one for the baby yet, Anastasia? What thought processes did you go through in choosing?

Anastasia: If I didn't have such a dumb name, Washburn Cum-mings would have liked me better.

Mother: What's wrong with your name? I think it's a lovely name.

Anastasia: You have to pay extra, for pete's sake, to have it sten-ciled on a tee shirt. There are too many letters. That's one thing wrong with it.

Father: Well, I'd be willing to fork over the extra money that a long name costs.

Anastasia: Look at me! I mean, look at my body.

Father: Not bad for ten years old. The legs are a little skinny, but I've seen worse.

Anastasia: I mean, look at my chest and picture my name across it.

Father: You know, Anastasia, my mind works verbally. Your mother is the one with the visual imagination. Why don't you have her look at your chest?

Narrator: Anastasia walks across the room to her mother, who is knitting clothing for the baby she is expecting.

Anastasia: Picture my name across my chest.

Mother: Wait 'til I finish this row. Okay, let me look. Yes. I see what you mean.

Anastasia: Into the armpits. Right? The letters would go right into my armpits!

Handling the Skills

The problem of perfecting and polishing skills in spelling, grammar, handwriting, and punctuation is minimized when chil-dren work cooperatively on something they want to do. Choice is an important factor in writing as well as in reading. Children need to know that there are many ways of responding in writing to the literature they read and hear. Poems, play scripts, essays, advertisements, book reviews, short stories, and interviews are some of the possibilities open to them. Production not perfection is the rule. Invented spelling is encouraged.

Writers need an audience. When children write together, the audience is ready-made. If they know that others are interested in their ideas, they will work harder to perfect the skills necessary for effective communication. When composing comes first, handwriting, punctuation, standard spellings, and the like are put in their place—one of importance in facilitating communication, but always as part of an editing process, coming after having something to say and someone to say it to.

Working with small groups and individuals, teachers give help with mechanical skills *where it is needed.* In every class there is such a wide range of language ability that it is a fruitless endeavor to drill spelling, punctuation, and all the rest with an entire class. The individual conference is more helpful; during it children can read aloud what they have written, a process that will reveal, among other things, how a piece should be punctuated.

Pre-writing sessions are all-important. In them necessary vocabulary is provided as required and ideas are brainstormed. Cooperative group efforts in composition assist the less able when they eventually write independently. Fully stimulated and prepared to write, children are ready to push their pencils, not chew them in frustration.

The practice of having children write a piece for the teacher to grade has no value as a learning experience. Confronted with a page of prose that seems to require major surgery, it is the rare teacher who can refrain from using the red pencil. As with reading, teachers need to note individual difficulties and work one on one or with small groups as required to help those who need special instruction and encouragement.

If a teacher does write a comment on a child's work, it should be in response to the ideas found there, to indicate that the writer has communicated something of an experience, interest, dream, or emotion. If, for example, a young writer tries to communicate, in halting prose, delight in a new pet, the teacher's comment responds to the effort: "Your cat sounds just like mine. I'd like to hear more about him."

Writing is a developmental process and a highly personal one. As a means of evaluation, examples of written work are filed in the children's portfolios. Self-evaluation is encouraged. In conferences, teachers and students note strengths and weaknesses in written work, and writers press on. What children need to know is that writing is a craft that continual effort may improve but never entirely perfect. The best professional writers struggle all their lives to express their thoughts precisely in contrary words that slip and slide out of their skilled control.

One's language is a part of oneself. To continually criticize children's language use is to make them feel inadequate as human beings. Writing especially is challenging and a little daunting for many students. More than training in technique, they require encouragement. Good teachers are like the poet Marie Ponsot, who for many years taught writing at Queens College. To her students she communicated her conviction that everyone can write. All they need to do is begin. Unintimidated, guided, and encouraged, countless students in her classes discovered that she was right. Expression through written words is not reserved only for professionals. The fulfillment that can come from writing is available to everyone at all levels of ability.

Nothing should be done to discourage children's efforts. Everything must be done to ensure that they experience some measure of the pleasure and satisfaction that can come through putting their feelings and ideas into written words.

Publication

Most children delight in seeing their work in print in classroom publications. An excellent form of publication that particularly appeals to children is the creation of their own simply bound books. These may be produced as class projects or as the work of individuals or small groups. They may be illustrated or decorated and include title pages, dedications, and tables of contents.

Young students enjoy creating shape books: a collection of tall tales in an appropriately shaped book, for example, or Thanksgiving poems in a book shaped like a pumpkin. Stories may be printed on charts or oak tag for room displays.

Class magazines or newspapers are excellent ways to publish compositions of all kinds. Another form of publication is a "talking" magazine or newspaper, with children recording on tape pieces they have composed. Use of the computer (word processor) takes the drudgery out of revising, editing, and preparing class newspapers and books. Even young children can prepare texts for printing.

FILM AND VIDEOTAPE
IN THE LITERATURE CURRICULUM

Movies and television especially are criticized for leading children away from reading and writing. Perhaps our best defense against the overpowering presence of film in children's lives is to incorporate it into literary studies. References to stories on film belong in discussions of printed stories and need to be welcomed and encouraged.

All the aspects of archetypal criticism that apply to printed stories apply as well to stories on film. Children will be encouraged to draw upon their experiences with film, in and out of school, in their discussions of literary principles. Just as they can learn to read printed stories perceptively, noting point of view, mood, tone, how characters develop and interrelate, and the like, so they can be taught to "read" film with greater perception.

Literature on film and literature in print have aspects in common, although each medium makes use of techniques unique to it. The film, with unusual juxtaposition of images, variations of angle, and length of shot, can create a metaphorical language of association without using words.

Shooting characters from below can make them appear overpowering and menacing. A long shot of an individual alone in a desolate place evokes feelings of loneliness. Darkness and shadow often symbolize the evil, menacing, or threatening; light and color are associated with their opposites. Images of landscapes and natural surroundings, as well as weather, create mood and atmosphere.

Film makers, as well as writers, must find ways to begin, develop, and end a story. The elements of story—character, setting, plot, theme, mood, tone—are all present in filmed narratives. Especially interesting is point of view, generally the camera's, which is usually omniscient and relatively objective.

The composition of filmed stories by students encompasses several aspects of the process of literary criticism. It involves a creative response as well as an analysis of the elements of story. If a printed story is to be adapted for filming, students need to be aware of the story in terms of its structure, deciding, for instance, what key scenes are essential to the re-creation of the story in movie form. They must note details of the characters' appearance to suggest appropriate casting and costuming. In reading or listening to the story, students must have visualized settings in order to design them for the film.

When the project involves the creation of an original movie, the storytellers must consider story structure: how and where it should begin, how and by whom the plot will be developed, how suspense will be maintained, how it will reach a satisfying ending.

Usually, the first step in the making of a film is the creation of a storyboard, a sequence of sketches that plan the story shot by shot, with instructions for the length and angle of each included in a caption. The storyboard has some obvious possibilities for teaching students to trace a sequence of events and for helping them to see how a story is formed.

Besides the regular fare of television and the movies, many excellent films and videos of quality children's literature have been created. Seeing these dramatizations is often motivation for children to read the books on which they are based. Some of these were seen as "Afternoon Specials" on ABC-TV in the 1970s and are still available in reruns. Fine books are adapted for television and aired on Reading Rainbow and Wonder Works. One example of an excellent adaptation is *The House of Dies Drear*, from the book by Virginia Hamilton (1968).

The use of filmed and printed literature together makes possible cross-media comparisons. The children will draw many conclusions about the unique characteristics of each medium. Films, for example, do not require descriptions of either the characters' appearance or the setting, since the viewer sees these details. In printed literature we can read what a character feels and thinks; film is more suited to showing the physical rather than the mental state of characters. Films reveal the characters' thoughts through their actions to a far greater degree than does the printed story.

Students will find it interesting to discuss the relative merits of each medium. In a classroom where printed literature is a lively art, no one will accept film as a substitute for it.

Postscript

Mathematics, social studies, and science all have their places in the curriculum. They are established as subjects of study: their content and methods of instruction receive serious consideration. It is still not so with literature. Yet literature, of all people's creations, is one of the greatest sources of nourishment for developing minds and imaginations.

It has the capacity to delight; it is meant to be enjoyed, and children in a time of illiteracy and aliteracy need to be convinced of its value. Literature is a humanistic study, and studies in the humanities are essential to our survival in a technological world where things can easily become more important than people. Literature has a civilizing influence. Because it deals with all human experience—our dreams and our nightmares—literature can show us both sides of the coin: what it means to be human and what it means to be inhumane.

Preoccupation with "teaching reading" has led us away from serious consideration of what it means to be truly literate. To become literate, children must read genuine literature from the beginning. Learning to read is learning to read literature, and learning to write—the other side of the literacy coin—is learning to write through literature. Literature *is* the language art. All other language "arts" develop from and through it.

At the elementary level, the literature itself, carefully chosen, must do most of the teaching. A light touch is required as we engage in literary criticism with young students. Literature is an art, and art is first of all to be experienced and savored. Aesthetic and creative responses to it must be nurtured. But experience and response are not enough. The study of literature takes place in school, and educators concern themselves with fostering growth and development. The growth of young critics depends on going beyond experiencing to reflecting on what literature is and how it works.

179

As defined here, literary criticism is an all-inclusive concept that includes experiencing literature, responding to it, reflecting on it, and creating it. Its practice does not depend on commercially prepared programs, narrow doctrines, or prescribed courses of study. No textbooks are necessary. What is needed to teach literary criticism is literature itself, genuine literature of all kinds and in great quantities. In this wealth of material all children will find some things that will compel them to listen, to read for themselves, to talk about what they read, and to try to create literature of their own. An informed, enthusiastic teacher is there to bring children and literature together, to listen, to ask the right questions, to inspire, and to nurture creative effort.

The development of language ability, whether reading or writing, is a cumulative development. Unlike other studies, it develops from the inside out. When words engage our feelings and imaginations, we are motivated to read them. When our feelings and imaginations are stimulated, we have a need to use language to express them.

Children in large numbers have not thrived on instructional diets that serve up imaginative literature only as dessert. These children turn to television to satisfy their desire for fantasy, their need to hear language that jingles, rhymes, and sings. For many of them reading is an onerous activity confined to classrooms.

With children, feeling comes first. They want to read what makes them laugh or cry, shiver or gasp. They need stories that reflect what they have felt but had no words to express. They need the thrill of imagining, of being in some character's shoes for a spine-tingling adventure. They deserve the delight that comes with hearing language that puns and plays. For children, reading must be equated with imagining, wondering, reacting feelingly. If it is not, we should not be surprised that they refuse to read.

Children must know words with power. This power is most evident in literature, writing by lovers of language who work at putting the best words in the best order for the greatest effect. Powerful words have magical powers: they can cast a spell to hold readers and listeners in thrall, and as this happens, a measure of their power transfers to each reader and listener. Sometimes discouraged, we may think that nothing less than magic can fight illiteracy and aliteracy. Then we are prepared. In words with power there is powerful magic. Our challenge is to see to it that children encounter these words.

Resources for Teachers

American Library Association
50 East Huron Street, Chicago, IL 60611. (800) 545–2433
The ALA provides a number of publications useful in choosing and evaluating children's books, among them *The Booklist, Picture Books for Children, Children's Books of International Interest, Let's Read Together: Books for Family Enjoyment, A Multimedia Approach to Children's Literature,* and *Beyond Fact: Nonfiction for Children and Young People. Top of the News* is an ALA periodical that discusses national and international issues relating to children's literature.

The ALA, which sponsors the annual Caldecott and Newbery awards, will supply for a nominal cost a list of the winners and runners-up (honor books) for both awards since their inception.

Bookbird: Literature for Children and Young People
Hermann Schaffstein
Verlag, D-4600, Dortland 1, Degginstr 93, Germany
This quarterly periodical on international literature for children is available in most libraries.

R. R. Bowker
121 Chanlon Road, New Providence, NJ 07974. (800) 521–8110
The public library is a good source for publications by Bowker, which include *Children's Books in Print, Subject Guide to Children's Books in Print, Paperbound Books for Young People: Kindergarten through Grade 12,* and *Best Books for Children: Preschool through Middle Grades.* The latter is an annotated listing of about 13,000 books. Also published by Bowker is *School Library Journal,* a periodical containing reviews of children's books.

Bulletin of the Center for Children's Books
Graduate Library School, University of Chicago
5801 Ellis Avenue, Chicago, IL 60637

This monthly bulletin contains reviews of new books, including comments on those not recommended.

CM: Canadian Materials for Schools and Libraries
Canadian Library Association
151 Sparks Street, Ottawa, Ontario, Canada KIP 583
Reviews books, films, games, and periodicals published in Canada.

Children and Books, 7th edition
Zena Sutherland and May Hill Arbuthnot
Chicago: Scott Foresman, 1986
A distinguished textbook of children's literature containing excellent bibliographies, discussion of various genres, and critical commentary on selected works.

The Children's Book Council
568 Broadway, Suite 404, New York, NY 10012. (212) 966–1990
The official sponsor and headquarters for National Children's Book Week, the Council is a nonprofit organization devoted to bringing children and good books together. A one-time charge puts a name permanently on the mailing list to receive a description of materials available for Book Week and the publication, *CBC Features,*which includes articles by authors and illustrators, topical bibliographies, and lists of sources of free materials such as posters, press sheets, and book marks. The Council, open to the public during business hours, maintains an examination collection of new books.

Christopher-Gordon Publishers, Inc.
480 Washington Street, Norwood, MA 02062. (617) 762–5577
Christopher-Gordon specializes in publications that deal with children's literature. *The New Advocate* is a quarterly journal of reviews and articles "for those involved with young people and their literature." *Perspectives,* another Christopher-Gordon periodical, deals with practical issues related to choosing and using books in the classroom.

Great Books Foundation
40 East Huron Street, Chicago, IL 60611–2782
(800) 222–5870 In Illinois: (312) 332–5870
Established in 1947, the Great Books Foundation is an independent, nonprofit educational corporation whose mission is to provide people of all ages with the opportunity to read, discuss, and learn from great works of literature. For a nominal fee, individuals may enroll in one of the two-day Basic Leader Training Courses offered regularly throughout the United States. Whether or not an individual wishes to lead official Great Books discussions, the training is helpful to anyone who helps children learn to

read literature. Central to the program is a method of discussion called "shared inquiry," in which participants and discussion leaders work together to formulate and discuss interpretive questions that focus on important problems of meaning in a literary work.

The Horn Book Magazine
14 Beacon Street, Boston, MA 02108
(800) 325–1170 In Massachusetts: (617) 227–1555

An entertaining and reliable way to learn what is happening in the world of children's books is through subscription to *The Horn Book Magazine*. Each issue contains articles by authors, illustrators, and critics; reviews of the best books published; and news about awards and conferences. The magazine publishes a selection of books and pamphlets on children's literature, including *The Horn Book Guide*, a biannual selection guide to children's and young adults' hardcover trade books.

International Reading Association
800 Barksdale Road, P.O. Box 8139, Newark, DE 19714–8139
(302) 731–1600

The IRA publishes a wide array of references for educators, librarians, and parents, as well as periodicals such as *The Reading Teacher*, which—like all IRA periodicals—comes with membership in the Association. Besides articles and features on teaching and learning, *The Reading Teacher* contains reviews of new children's books.

National Council of Teachers of English
1111 Kenyon Road, Urbana, IL 61801
(800) 369–NCTE In Illinois (217) 328–3870

Membership in the NCTE, which sponsors professional conferences and publishes books and periodicals on the teaching of English, is an excellent way to stay current on matters of importance in the field of English teaching. Subscription to *Language Arts*, a periodical published September through April and including book reviews, articles by teachers, and Council information, is available as part of membership. The NCTE publishes regularly updated versions of comprehensive booklists: *Adventuring with Books* (pre-K through Grade 6), *Your Reading* (middle school/junior high), *Books for You* (senior high), and *High Interest/Easy Reading* (Junior/senior high reluctant readers). Another useful reference available through the NCTE is *Reading Ladders for Human Relations*, which features annotated reviews of children's books under such headings as "Growing into Self," "Interacting in Groups," and "Coping in a Changing World."

New York Public Library, Children's Services
8 East 40th Street, New York, NY 10016. (212) 340–0906

A number of pamphlets and booklists are available from the children's services division of the New York Public Library, notably *The Black Experience in Children's Books* and *Libros en español*.

The Read-Aloud Handbook
Jim Trelease, New York: Penguin Books, 1985
This handbook contains a well-reasoned rationale for reading aloud and lists of books especially suited for the purpose. Another helpful book on the subject is *For Reading Out Loud! A Guide to Sharing Books with Children*, by Margaret Mary Kimmel and Elizabeth Segel, New York: Dell, 1984.

Teachers Applying Whole Language
Whole Language Umbrella, P.O. Box 721326, Berkley, MI 48072
The Whole Language Umbrella newsletter is published three times each school year by the Detroit TAWL group for members of the Whole Language Umbrella, a confederation of whole-language teacher support groups. For information on membership, contact Debbie Manning, 4848 N. Fruit, Fresno, CA 93705.

Teachers Networking: The Whole Language Newsletter, another publication devoted to whole-language issues, is published by Richard C. Owen Publishers Inc., Box 585, Katonah, NY 10536.

Weston Woods
Weston, CT 06883–9989. (800) 243–5020
The Weston Woods catalogue is entitled *Children's Literature in the Audiovisual Media*, reflecting this company's focus on videocassettes, motion pictures, sound filmstrips, and recordings of children's literature. Quality picture books are superbly rendered on film and filmstrip. Kits of recordings with accompanying booklets are designed for independent reading/listening.

The H. W. Wilson Company
950 University Avenue, Bronx, NY 10452. (212) 588–8400
The Wilson Company produces a wide variety of reference materials for libraries. Among them is the Wilson *Library Bulletin*, which features a monthly column of reviews of children's books, and *Children's Catalog*, a listing of recent children's books issued every 5 years. Also available through Wilson is an *Index to Poetry for Children and Young People*, in several volumes. Poems are indexed by title, first line, author, and subject.

Literary References

Alexander, Lloyd. (1982). *The kestrel.* New York: Dutton.

Aliki. (1989). *The King's day: Louis XIV of France.* New York: Crowell.

Andersen, Hans Christian. (1974). *The complete fairy tales and stories.* Translated from the Danish by Erik Haugaard. Garden City, NY: Doubleday.

Armstrong, William. (1969). *Sounder.* New York: Harper & Row.

Atwater, Richard & Florence. (1938). *Mr. Popper's penguins.* Boston: Little, Brown.

Babbitt, Natalie. (1977). *The eyes of the Amaryllis.* New York: Farrar, Straus & Giroux.

Bauer, Marian D. (1986). *On my honor.* New York: Clarion.

Baylor, Byrd. (1974). *Everybody needs a rock.* Illustrated by Peter Parnall. New York: Macmillan.

Bedard, Michael. (1987). *A darker magic.* New York: Atheneum.

Brittain, Bill. (1984). *The wish giver.* New York: Harper & Row.

Brittain, Bill. (1987). *Dr. Dread's wagon of wonders.* New York: Harper & Row.

Brooke, Rupert. (1915). *The collected poems of Rupert Brooke.* London: John Lane.

Byars, Betsy. (1981a). *The Cybil war.* New York: Viking.

Byars, Betsy. (1981b). *The winged colt of Casa Mia.* New York: Avon.

Byars, Betsy. (1987). *The Blossoms and the green phantoms.* New York: Delacorte.

Carroll, Lewis. (1988). *Alice's adventures in wonderland.* Illustrated by Anthony Browne. New York: Knopf. (Original work published 1865)

Chase, Richard. (1943). *Jack tales.* Boston: Houghton Mifflin.

Christopher, John. (1967). *The white mountains.* New York: Macmillan.

Cleary, Beverly. (1983). *Dear Mr. Henshaw.* New York: Morrow.

Clifford, Eth. (1981). *Help! I'm a prisoner in the library.* New York: Dell.

Conrad, Pam. (1986). *Holding me here.* New York: Harper & Row.

Cooper, Susan. (1973). *The dark is rising.* New York: Atheneum.

Cormier, Robert. (1983). *The bumblebee flies anyway.* New York: Knopf.

Cunningham, Julia. (1965). *Dorp dead.* New York: Pantheon.

De la Mare, Walter. (1983). *Molly Whuppie.* New York: Farrar, Straus & Giroux.

Dickens, Charles. (1952). *A Christmas carol.* Illustrated by Arthur Rackham. New York: Lippincott. (Original work published 1843)

DuBois, William Pene. (1947). *The twenty-one balloons.* New York: Viking.

Ehrlich, Amy. (1988). *Where it stops nobody knows.* New York: Dial.

Emberley, Barbara, Adapter. (1967). *Drummer Hoff.* Illustrated by Ed Emberley. Englewood Cliffs, NJ: Prentice-Hall.

Farley, Walter. (1941). *The black stallion.* New York: Random House.

Fitzhugh, Louise. (1974). *Nobody's family is going to change.* New York: Farrar, Straus & Giroux.

Fleischman, Sid. (1987). *The whipping boy.* New York: Greenwillow.

Frost, Robert. (1978). "Stopping by woods on a snowy evening." Illustrated by Susan Jeffers. New York: Dutton.

Gág, Wanda. (1928). *Millions of cats.* New York: Coward McCann.

Gardiner, John. (1980). *Stone Fox.* New York: Crowell.

Garner, Alan. (1968). *The owl service.* New York: Walck.

Gramatky, Hardie. (1939). *Little Toot.* New York: Putnam.

Greenfield, Eloise. (1978). *Honey, I love and other love poems.* New York: Harper & Row.

Grimm, Jakob & Wilhelm. (1886/1972). *Snow White and the seven dwarfs.* Translated by Randell Jarrell and illustrated by Nancy Berkert. New York: Farrar, Straus & Giroux.

Hamilton, Virginia. (1968). *The house of Dies Drear.* New York: Macmillan.

Heide, Florence. (1971). *The shrinking of Treehorn.* New York: Holiday House.

Henry, Marguerite. (1948). *King of the wind.* Chicago: Rand McNally.

Hoban, Russell. (1967). *The mouse and his child.* London: Faber and Faber.

Hodges, Margaret. (1984). *Saint George and the dragon.* Boston: Little, Brown.

Holm, Ann. (1965, 1984). *North to freedom.* Translated by L. W. Kingsland. New York: Harcourt Brace Jovanovich.

Holman, Felice. (1974). *Slake's limbo.* New York: Charles Scribner's Sons.

Hughes, Monica. (1981). *The keeper of the Isis light.* New York: Atheneum.

Hutchins, Pat. (1968). *Rosie's walk.* New York: Macmillan.

Keats, Ezra Jack. (1962). *The snowy day.* New York: Viking.

Keats, John. (1956). *Keats: Poetical works.* Edited by H. W. Garrod. London: Oxford University Press.

Kellogg, Steven. (1985). *Chicken Little.* Illustrated by the author. New York: Morrow.

Kipling, Rudyard. (1987). *Just-so stories.* Illustrated by Safaya Salter. New York: Holt. (Original work published 1902)

Langton, Jane. (1980). *The fledgling.* New York: Harper & Row.

Lauber, Patricia. (1989). *The news about dinosaurs.* New York: Bradbury.

Le Guin, Ursula. (1968). *A wizard of Earthsea.* Illustrated by Ruth Robbins. New York: Parnassus.

Lively, Penelope. (1973). *The ghost of Thomas Kempe.* New York: Dutton.

Lowry, Lois. (1979). *Anastasia Krupnik.* Boston: Houghton Mifflin.

Lowry, Lois. (1986). *Anastasia has the answers.* Boston: Houghton Mifflin.

MacLachlan, Patricia. (1986). *Sarah, plain and tall.* New York: Harper & Row.

Martin, Bill & Archambault, John. (1989). *Chicka chicka boom boom.* New York: Simon and Schuster.

Maruki, Toshi. (1980). *Hiroshima no pika.* New York: Lothrop, Lee & Shepard.

Mayne, William. (1990). *Antar and the eagles.* New York: Delacorte.

Mazer, Norma Fox. (1982). *Mrs. Fish, Ape, and me, the dump queen.* New York: Avon.

McCord, David. (1974). *One at a time.* Boston: Little, Brown.

McDermott, Gerald. (1975). *The stonecutter.* New York: Viking.

McDermott, Gerald. (1977). *The voyage of Osiris: A myth of ancient Egypt.* New York: Viking.

McDermott, Gerald. (1978). *Arrow to the sun.* New York: Puffin.

McGovern, Ann. (1977). *Wanted dead or alive: The story of Harriet Tubman.* New York: Scholastic.

McKinley, Robin. (1985). *The hero and the crown.* New York: Greenwillow.

Merriam, Eve. (1965). *Do you want to see something?* New York: Scholastic.

Merriam, Eve. (1974). *Out loud.* New York: Atheneum.

Merrill, Jean. (1964). *The pushcart war.* New York: Young Scott.

Millay, Edna St. Vincent. (1924). *The harp-weaver and other poems.* New York: Harper and Brothers.

Milne, A. A. (1924). *When we were very young.* New York: Dutton.

Neil, Philip. (1986). *Drakestail visits the king.* New York: Philomel.

Norton, Mary. (1953). *The borrowers.* New York: Harcourt Brace Jovanovich.

Nostlinger, Christine. (1977). *Konrad.* Translated by Anthea Bell. New York: Watts.

Noyes, Alfred. (1902). *Collected poems of Alfred Noyes.* New York: Lippincott.

O'Dell, Scott. (1970). *Sing down the moon.* Boston: Houghton Mifflin.

O'Keefe, Susan H. (1989). *One hungry monster: A counting book in rhyme.* Boston: Little, Brown.

Osborne, Mary Pope. (1987). *Beauty and the beast.* Illustrated by Winslow Pels. New York: Scholastic.

Paterson, Katherine. (1977). *Bridge to Terabithia.* New York: Crowell.

Paterson, Katherine. (1978). *The great Gilly Hopkins.* New York: Crowell.

Paulsen, Gary. (1985). *Dogsong.* New York: Bradbury.

Paulsen, Gary. (1988). *Hatchet.* New York: Bradbury.

Peck, Richard. (1977). *Are you in the house alone?* New York: Dell.

Peck, Richard. (1983). *The dreadful future of Blossom Culp.* New York: Delacorte.

Perrault, Charles. (1981). *Cinderella.* Illustrated by Marcia Brown. New York: Macmillan.

Perrault, Charles. (1990). *Puss in boots.* Illustrated by Fred Marcellino. New York; Farrar, Straus & Giroux.

Pfeffer, Susan. (1987). *The year without Michael.* New York: Bantam.

Picard, Barbara. (1966). *One is one.* New York: Holt, Rinehart and Winston.

Pinkwater, Manus. (1976). *Lizard music.* New York: Dodd, Mead.

Potter, Beatrix. (1902). *The tale of Peter Rabbit.* London: Warne.

Potter, Beatrix. (1912). *The tale of Mr. Tod.* London: Warne.

Ritchie, Alice. (1949). *The treasure of Li Po.* New York: Harcourt Brace Jovanovich.

Sachs, Marilyn. (1971). *The bears' house.* New York: Doubleday.

Saltman, Judith. (1985). *The Riverside anthology of children's literature* (6th ed.). Boston; Houghton Mifflin.

Sawyer, Ruth. (1936). The flea in *Picture tales from Spain.* New York: Lippincott.

Sebestyen, Ouida. (1979). *Words by heart.* Boston: Little, Brown.

Sebestyen, Ouida. (1988). *The girl in the box.* Boston: Little, Brown.

Sendak, Maurice. (1963). *Where the wild things are.* New York: Harper & Row.

Sendak, Maurice. (1988). *Dear Mili.* New York: Farrar, Straus & Giroux.

Seuss, Dr. (1938). *The 500 hats of Bartholomew Cubbins.* New York: Random House.

Siebert, Diane. (1989). *Heartland.* New York: Crowell.

Sleator, William. (1984). *Interstellar pig.* New York: Dutton.

Slobodkina, Esphyr. (1947). *Caps for sale.* New York: Scott.

Smith, Robert. (1972). *Chocolate fever.* New York: Dell.

Speare, Elizabeth. (1983). *The sign of the beaver.* Boston: Houghton Mifflin.

Sperry, Armstrong. (1940). *Call it courage.* New York: Macmillan.

Steig, William. (1969). *Sylvester and the magic pebble.* New York: Simon and Schuster.

Steig, William. (1972). *Dominic.* New York: Farrar, Straus & Giroux.

Steig, William. (1986). *Brave Irene.* New York: Farrar, Straus & Giroux.

Steinbeck, John. (1976). *The acts of King Arthur and his noble knights.* New York: Farrar, Straus & Giroux.

Steptoe, John. (1987). *Mufaro's beautiful daughters.* New York: Lothrop Lee & Shepard.

Sterling, Dorothy. (1954). *Freedom train: The story of Harriet Tubman.* New York: Doubleday.

Stone, A. Harris. (1967). *The last free bird.* Englewood Cliffs, NJ: Prentice-Hall.

Swift, Jonathan. (1985). *Gulliver's travels.* New York: Avenel Books. (Original work published 1726).

Tsuchiya, Yukio. (1988). *Faithful elephants.* Translated by Tomoko Tsuchiya Dykes. Boston: Houghton Mifflin.

Updike, John. (1975). *Picked-up pieces.* New York: Alfred Knopf.

Van Allsburg, Chris. (1981). *Jumanji.* Boston: Houghton Mifflin.

Voight, Cynthia. (1982). *Dicey's song.* New York: Atheneum.

White, E. B. (1952). *Charlotte's web.* New York: Harper & Row.

White, E. B. (1970). *The trumpet of the swan.* New York: Harper & Row.

Wolfe, Humbert. (1962). "The gray squirrel." In Louis Untermeyer (Ed.), *Modern British poetry* (7th rev. ed.). New York: Harcourt Brace Jovanovich.

Yashima, Taro. (1976). Crow boy. New York: Puffin.

Yolen, Jane. (1984). *Sleeping ugly.* New York: Coward-McCann.

Zelinsky, Paul O. (1986). *Rumpelstiltskin.* New York: Dutton.

Zindel, Paul. (1968). *The Pigman.* New York: Harper & Row.

Zindel, Paul. (1980). *The Pigman's legacy.* New York: Harper & Row.

General References

Anderson, R. C., Heibert, E. H., Scott, J. A., & Wilkinson, I. A. G. (1985). *Becoming a nation of readers: The report of the Commission on Reading.* Washington, DC: National Institute of Education.

Applebee, Arthur. (1978). *The child's concept of story.* Chicago: University of Chicago Press.

Ashton-Warner, Sylvia. (1964). *Teacher.* New York: Bantam Books.

Atwell, Nancie. (1987). *In the middle.* Portsmouth, NH: Heinemann.

Babbitt, Natalie. (1990). Protecting children's literature. *Horn Book Magazine,* November/December, 696–703.

Baghban, Marcia. (1984). *Our daughter learns to read and write.* Newark, DE: International Reading Association.

Barbe, Walter. (1961). *Personalized reading instruction.* Englewood Cliffs, NJ: Prentice-Hall.

Bennett, Jill. (1979). *Learning to read with picture books* (3rd ed.). Stroud, England: The Thimble Press.

Bettleheim, Bruno. (1976). *The uses of enchantment: Meaning and importance of fairy tales.* New York: Knopf.

Calkins, Lucy. (1986). *The art of teaching writing.* Portsmouth, NH: Heinemann.

Carr, J. (1982). *Beyond fact.* Chicago: American Library Association.

Carr, J. (1987). Filling vases, lighting fires. *The Horn Book Magazine, 63,* 710–713.

Chomsky, Carol. (1972). Stages in language development and reading exposure. *Harvard Educational Review, 42,* 1–33.

Chomsky, Carol. (1978). When you still can't read in third grade: After decoding, what? In *What research has to say about reading instruction* (pp. 13–30). Newark, DE: International Reading Association.

Chomsky, Noam. (1957). *Syntactic structures.* The Hague: Mouton.

Clarke, Margaret. (1976). *Young fluent readers: What can they teach us?* London: Heinemann.

Clay, Marie. (1980). *Reading: The patterning of complex behavior* (2nd ed.). Auckland, Australia: Heinemann.

Cohen, Dorothy. (1968). The effect of literature on vocabulary and reading achievement. *Elementary English, 45,* 209–213, 217.

193

Cohen, Elizabeth. (1986). *Designing group work.* New York: Teachers College Press.

Coles, Robert. (1989). *The call of stories.* Boston: Houghton Mifflin.

Cormier, Robert. (1986). Books remembered. *Children's Book Council Features, 40*(2), unpaged.

Crook, Patricia, & Lehman, Barbara. (1991). Themes for two voices: Children's fiction and nonfiction as "whole literature." *Language Arts, 68,* 34–41.

Culler, Jonathan. (1978). *The pursuit of signs.* London: Routledge and Kegan Paul.

Cullinan, Bernice. (1989). *Literature and the child* (2nd ed.). New York: Harcourt Brace Jovanovich.

Cullinan, Bernice, Jagger, Angela, & Strickland, Dorothy. (1974). Language expansion for black children in the primary grades: A research report. *Young Children, 29,* 98–112.

Curran, Karen. (1987). *A study of the effect on children's writing of selected folk tales read aloud.* Unpublished Master of Education paper, School of Education, Queens College of the City University of New York.

Dressel, Janice. (1988). Critical thinking and the perception of aesthetic form. *Language Arts, 65,* 567–572.

Durkin, Dolores. (1966). *Children who read early.* New York: Teachers College Press.

Eckhoff, Barbara. (1983). How reading affects children's writing. *Language Arts, 60,* 607–616.

Eldredge, J. Lloyd, & Butterfield, Dennie. (1986). Alternatives to traditional reading instruction. *The Reading Teacher, 40,* 32–37.

Fitzgerald, Regina. (1986). *Children's poetry preferences in the fifth grade.* Unpublished Master of Education paper, School of Education, Queens College of the City University of New York.

Fleming, Carolyn. (1981). *Small is heroic.* Unpublished master's thesis submitted for the degree of Master of Arts, School of Humanities, The Flinders University of South Australia.

Fox, C. (1983). Talking like a book: Young children's oral monologues. In M. Meek (Ed.), *Opening moves: Work in progress in the study of children's language development.* London: University of London Institute of Education.

Fox, C. (1985). The book that talks. *Language Arts, 62*(4), 374–384.

Frye, Northrop. (1956). Poetry. *University of Toronto Quarterly, 25,* 290–304.

Frye, Northrop. (1957). *Anatomy of criticism: Four essays.* Princeton, NJ: Princeton University Press.

Frye, Northrop. (1963a). *The educated imagination.* Toronto: Canadian Broadcasting Corporation.

Frye, Northrop. (1963b). *The well-tempered critic.* Bloomington: Indiana University Press.

Frye, Northrop. (1970). *The stubborn structure: Essays on criticism and society.* Ithaca: Cornell University Press.

Frye, Northrop. (1976a). *The secular scripture.* Cambridge, MA: Harvard University Press.

Frye, Northrop. (1976b). *Spiritus mundi.* Bloomington: Indiana University Press.

Frye, Northrop. (1982). *The great code: The Bible and literature.* New York: Harcourt Brace Jovanovich.

Frye, Northrop. (1988). *On education.* Markham, Ontario: Fitzhenry and Whiteside.

Frye, Northrop. (1990). *Words with power: Being a second study of the Bible and literature.* New York: Harcourt Brace Jovanovich.

Gallo, Donald. (Ed.). (1977). Teaching writing: Advice from the professionals. *Connecticut English Journal, 8(2),* entire issue.

Geller, Linda G. (1985). *Wordplay and language learning for children.* Urbana, IL: National Council of Teachers of English.

Goodman, Kenneth. (1968). The psycholinguistic nature of the reading process. In Kenneth Goodman (Ed.), *The psycholinguistic nature of the reading process.* Detroit: Wayne State University Press.

Goodman, Kenneth & Yetta. (1979). Learning to read is natural. In L. B. Resnick & P. A. Weaver (Eds.), *Theory and practice of early reading.* Hillsdale, NJ: Erlbaum.

Goodman, Kenneth, Shannon, P., Freeman, Y., & Murphy, S. (1988). *Report card on basal readers.* Katonah, NY: Richard Owen.

Goodman, Yetta. (1989). Evaluation in whole language classrooms. In *Teachers Networking, 9(4),* Katonah, NY: Richard Owen.

Goodman, Yetta, Watson, Dorothy, & Burke, Carolyn. (1987). *Reading miscue inventory: Alternative procedures.* Katonah, NY: Richard Owen.

Graves, Donald. (1983). *Writing: Teachers and children at work.* Portsmouth, NH: Heinemann.

Guthrie, J. (1981). Reading in New Zealand: Achievement, volume. *Reading Research Quarterly, 17,* 6–17.

Halliday, M. A. K. (1975). *Learning how to mean: Explorations in the development of language.* London: Edward Arnold.

Hardy, Barbara. (1977). Towards a poetics of fiction: An approach through narrative. In M. Meek, A. Warlow, & G. Barton (Eds.), *The cool web: The pattern of children's reading* (pp. 12–23). New York: Atheneum.

Harste, J., Woodward, V., & Burke, C. (1984). *Language stories and literacy lessons.* Portsmouth, NH: Heinemann.

Heard, Georgia. (1989). *For the good of the earth and the sun: Teaching poetry.* Portsmouth, NH: Heinemann.

Heath, Shirley B. (1985). Literacy or literate skills? Considerations for ESL/EFL learners. In P. Larson, E. Judd, & D. Messerschmitt (Eds.), *On TESOL.* Washington, DC: TESOL.

Henke, Linda. (1988). Beyond basal reading: A district's commitment to change. *The New Advocate, 1(1),* 42–51.

Hickman, Janet. (1986). Children's response to literature. *Language Arts, 63,* 2.

Holdaway, Don. (1979). *The foundations of literacy.* Auckland, Australia: Scholastic.

Holdaway, Don. (1984). *Stability and change in literacy learning.* Portsmouth, NH: Heinemann.

Horrocks, Lorraine. (1986). *Children's poetry preferences in the first grade.* Unpublished Master of Education paper, School of Education, Queens College of the City University of New York.

Huck, Charlotte. (1961). *Children's literature in the elementary school* (1st ed.). New York: Holt.

Huck, Charlotte, Hepler, Susan, & Hickman, Janet. (1987). *Children's literature in the elementary school* (4th ed.). New York: Holt.

Jacobs, Leland. (1965). *Using literature with young children.* New York: Teachers College Press.

Koch, Kenneth. (1970). *Wishes, lies, and dreams.* New York: Chelsea House.

Koeller, Shirley. (1981). 25 years advocating children's literature in the reading program. *The Reading Teacher, 34,* 552–556.

Larrick, Nancy. (1987). Illiteracy starts too soon. *Phi Delta Kappan, 69,* 184–189.

Meek, Margaret. (1982). *Learning to read.* Portsmouth, NH: Heinemann.

Miller, George A. (1962). Some psychological studies of grammar. *American Psychologist, 17,* 748–762.

Moss, Joy. (1984). *Focus units in literature.* Urbana, IL: National Council of Teachers in English.

Moynagh, Ann. (1986). *The effects of book talks on children's reading habits.* Unpublished Master of Education paper, School of Education, Queens College of the City University of New York.

Odland, Norine. (1969). *Teaching literature in the elementary school.* Urbana, IL: National Council of Teachers of English.

Opie, Iona & Peter. (1959). *The lore and language of school children.* New York: Oxford University Press.

Padgett, Ron. (1987). *Handbook of poetic forms.* New York: Teachers and Writers Collaborative.

Paterson, Katherine. (1989). *The spying heart: More thoughts on reading and writing books for children.* New York: Dutton.

Rigg, Pat, & Allen, Virginia (Eds.). (1989). *When they don't all speak English: Integrating the ESL student into the regular classroom.* Urbana, IL: National Council of Teachers of English.

Rogovin, Phyllis. (1985). *Poetic devices in children's speech.* Unpublished Master of Education paper, School of Education, Queens College of the City University of New York.

Rosen, Harold. (1985). *Stories and meanings.* Sheffield, England: National Association for the Teaching of English.

Rosen, Harold. (1986). The importance of story. *Language Arts, 63*(3), 226–237.

Rosenblatt, Louise. (1938). *Literature as exploration.* New York: Appleton-Century.

Rosenblatt, Louise. (1978). *The reader, the text, the poem: The transactional theory of the literary work.* Carbondale: Southern Illinois University Press.

Seashore, C. E. (Ed.). (1919). Fourth report of the Committee on Economy of Time in Education. In *18th Yearbook of the National Society for the Study of Education* (Part 2). Chicago: University of Chicago Press.

Shuy, Roger. (1981). A holistic view of language. *Research in the Teaching of English, 15*(2), 101–111.

Skinner, B. F. (1957). *Verbal behavior.* New York: Appleton-Century.

Sloan, Glenna. (1972). A delicate balance. *Elementary English,* April, 596–599.

Sloan, Glenna. (1974). The education of the imagination. *Elementary English, 51*(7), 977–982.

Sloan, Glenna. (1975). *The child as critic* (1st ed.). New York: Teachers College Press.

Sloan, Glenna. (1980). Developing literacy through literature. *The Reading Teacher, 34*(2), 132–136.

Sloan, Glenna. (1981). Eve Merriam. *Language Arts, 58*(8), 957–964.

Sloan, Glenna. (1984). *The child as critic* (2nd ed.). New York: Teachers College Press.

Sloan, Glenna. (1988). *Literature-based instruction in six elementary classrooms.* Unpublished research study.

Smith, Frank. (1973). *Psycholinguistics and reading.* New York: Holt.

Smith, Frank. (1978). *Understanding reading* (2nd ed.). New York: Holt.

Smith, Frank. (1983). *Essays into literacy.* Portsmouth, NH: Heinemann.

Smith, Frank. (1986). *Insult to intelligence: The bureaucratic invasion of our classrooms.* New York: Arbor House.

Snow, Charles P. (1959). *The two cultures and the scientific revolution.* New York: Cambridge University Press.

Spack, Ruth. (1985). Literature, reading, writing, and ESL: Bridging the gaps. *TESOL Quarterly, 19,* 5–14.

Stein, N., & Trabasso, T. (1982). What's in a story: An approach to comprehension and instruction. In R. Glacer (Ed.). *Advances in instructional psychology* (Vol. 2, pp. 213–254). Hillsdale, NJ: Erlbaum.

Terry, Ann. (1974). *Children's poetry preferences.* Urbana, IL: National Council of Teachers of English.

Tunnell, Michael. (1986). The natural act of reading: An affective approach. *The Advocate, 5,* 156–64.

Tyler, Ralph. (1977). Reading aloud: Is it time for a revival? *Bookviews, 1,* 16–20.

Veatch, Jeanette. (1959). *Individualizing your reading program.* New York: Putnam.

Veatch, Jeanette. (1968). *How to teach reading with children's books.* Katonah, NY: Richard Owen.

Walcutt, Charles, & McCracken, Glenn. (1981). *Jumping up.* Lippincott Basic Reading. New York: Lippincott.

Walmsley, Sean A., & Walp, Trudy P. (1989). Teaching literature in elementary school. Report Series 1.3. Center for the Learning and Teaching of Literature. Albany: State University of New York.

Wells, Gordon. (1982). Story reading and the development of symbolic skills. *Australian Journal of Reading, 5,* 3.

Wells, Gordon. (1986). *The meaning makers: Children learning language and using language to learn.* Portsmouth, NH: Heinemann.

Wilkinson, A. (1971). *The foundations of language.* New York: Oxford University Press.

Willinsky, John. (in press). *The triumph of literature/The fate of literacy.* New York: Teachers College Press.

Wolsch, Robert. (1970). *Poetic composition through the grades.* New York: Teachers College Press.

Zarnowski, Myra. (1990). *Learning about biographies: A reading-and-writing approach for children.* Urbana, IL: National Council of Teachers of English.

Index

About the Author

Glenna Sloan earned a B.A. from the University of Toronto; M.A. and doctoral degrees from Teachers College, Columbia University, where she studied children's literature with Leland B. Jacobs; and an associate's diploma (ARCT) in Speech and Drama from the Royal Conservatory of Music of Toronto. A specialist in reading, language arts, and children's literature, Dr. Sloan taught for 16 years in elementary and junior high schools. She is currently Professor of Education in the Department of Elementary and Early Childhood Education at Queens College of the City University of New York.

In addition to *The Child as Critic,* she has published articles in professional journals, a series on reading and study skills for junior high school students, a sixth-grade language arts text, and a novel for young people. She was author and consultant for the Harcourt Brace Jovanovich series, *Literature: Uses of the Imagination.* A member of the National Council of Teachers of English, Dr. Sloan serves on the Council's Committee on Literature-based Language Arts Instruction and is past Chair of the NCTE Poetry Award Committee. As a consultant for school systems, she evaluates programs and designs and leads in-service seminars and workshops for teachers.